"The montage edits the film material (which consists of very long or very short fragments and as many take sequences and possible subjective perspectives) just as death edits life."

Pier Paolo Pasolini, *Notes on the Take Sequences, 1967*

The Pasolini family moves to Parma, and continues to move often until 1936, due to Carlo's military job

The family begins taking summer vacations in Casarsa della Delizia, in Friuli, where Susanna is from

Pier Paolo Pasolini is born in Bologna on March 5, the son of infantry officer Carlo Alberto Pasolini and elementary school teacher Susanna Colussi

Birth of brother Guido, in Belluno

1922

1923

1924

1925

1926

1927

Fearing a Fascist putsch, King Vittorio Emanuele III appoints Fascist party leader Benito Mussolini *(Il Duce)* prime minister on October 31

Founding of the USSR

Maria Callas born in New York

Murder of Socialist opposition politician Giacomo Matteotti; the Fascist party (PNF) consolidates its power

Mussolini bans the Italian Communist Party (PCI) and has the party leadership, including Antonio Gramsci, arrested

Starts high school *(liceo)*
in Conegliano, later moving
to Cremona and Reggio
Emilia

Pasolini writes his first
poems at the age of seven

1928   **1929**   **1930**   **1931**   **1932**   **1933**

Italy becomes a dictatorship

Under the Lateran Treaty,
the Vatican and Italy
recognize each other as
sovereign states for the first
time in fifty-eight years

The family returns
to Bologna

1934   **1935**   **1936**   **1937**   **1938**   **1939**

1936

Mussolini announces the
Rome-Berlin axis, an alliance
with Adolf Hitler

Italy occupies Abyssinia

1937

Italy leaves the League of
Nations

Communist leader Antonio
Gramsci (born in 1891) dies
in prison

1939

Italy enters World War II
with the invasion of Albania

Mussolini declares war on
France and Britain

Writes PhD thesis on poet
Giovanni Pascoli; his art
history thesis on the contemporary Italian paintings of
Carlo Carrà, Filippo De Pisis,
and Giorgio Morandi gets
lost during the war

With his mother, Pasolini
begins teaching students in
Casarsa

Takes a teaching job at a
junior high school near
Casarsa

Pasolini takes graduation
exams in Bologna

Enrolls at the University of
Bologna, where he studies
art history, literature, and
romance languages

Founding of *Eredi* and *Il
setaccio* journals

Poesie a Casarsa (first
volume of lyric poetry,
written in Friulian dialect)

Family moves to Casarsa as
the war reaches Bologna

Brief military service until
the armistice between the
Allies and Italy

Academiuta di lenga furlana
established, a center for
the promotion of Friulian
literature and culture

I Turcs tal Friùl (a play
written in Friulian dialect)

Brother Guido is murdered
by Communist partisans

Father returns from the war

Diarii (Diaries)

First drawings

1940

1941

1942

1943

1944

1945

Fall and arrest of Mussolini

Military regime under Pietro
Badoglio, armistice with the
United States

German troops occupy Italy,
liberate Mussolini, and
establish the radical Fascist
Repubblica Sociale Italiana
(or Republic of Salò) under
his leadership

Capture and execution of
Mussolini by partisans

Falls in love with Tonuti
Spagnol, a *contadino*
(peasant)

Charged with "obscene acts";
his teaching appointment
is brought to an end and he
is expelled from the Com-
munist Party

Hastily moves to Rome with
his mother

Slowly begins a new life in
Rome

Takes an interest in the
life of the city's poorer
neighborhoods, known as
the *borgate*

Begins to be regularly
published in various
newspapers

Carlo Alberto joins the
family in Rome

Teaches at a private church
school in Ciampino, in Rome

Makes friends with boys
from the *borgate*, notably
Sergio Citti

Works for a literary program
on the radio

Start of his friendship with
painter Giuseppe Zigaina

I pianti (poems)

Dov'è la mia patria (poems)

Pasolini becomes politically
active in the Friuli region;
studies the writings of
Antonio Gramsci; joins the
Communist Party (PCI)

1946   1947   1948   1949   1950   1951

Italy becomes a republic
following a popular vote

The first republican
constitution enacted in Italy

Agrarian crisis in Italy,
agricultural workers strike,
land occupied by force

Collaborates on the screenplay of the film *Il prigioniero della montagna* by Luis Trenker

Publication of *Ragazzi di vita* causes scandal; first legal proceedings take place

Founding of *Officina* literary magazine

Friendship develops with writers Elsa Morante and Alberto Moravia

Ragazzi di vita | The Ragazzi (novel)

Canzoniere italiano (collection of Italian folk songs)

Poesia dialettale del Novecento (anthology of poems in dialect)

Collaborates with Giorgio Bassani on the screenplay of *La donna del fiume*

Tal còur di un frut (poems)

Dal diario (poems)

La meglio gioventù (poems)

Il canto popolare (collection of songs)

Collaborates on the screenplay of the film *Le notti di Cabiria* (Nights of Cabiria) by Federico Fellini

Awarded the Viareggio Prize for *Le ceneri di Gramsci*

Le ceneri di Gramsci | The Ashes of Gramsci (poems)

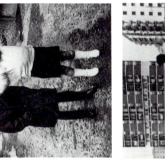

1952

1953

1954

1955

1956

1957

First major international television broadcast in Europe: the coronation of Queen Elizabeth II

USA and USSR both possess a hydrogen bomb

Uprising in East Germany (June 17)

Maria Callas plays Medea in Cherubini's opera at La Scala, in Milan

Hungarian uprising

Habib Bourguiba becomes the first president of an independent Tunisi

Algeria becomes independent

First Russian Sputnik launched into space

Friendship with Laura Betti begins

Pasolini's father dies

L'usignolo della chiesa cattolica | The Nightingale of the Catholic Church (poems)

Prosecuted for an epigram about Pope Pius XII in *Officina*

Una vita violenta | A Violent Life (novel)

La notte brava | Bad Girls Don't Cry / On Any Street (screenplay for *Ragazzi di vita*)

Writes a weekly column in the Communist newspaper *Vie nuove* (until 1965)

Prosecuted several times for obscenities in the novel *Una vita violenta*

First trip to India (winter)

Roma 1950 (diaries)

Sonetto primaverile (poems)

Donne di Roma (prose)

Passione e ideologia (collection of essays)

La poesia popolare italiana (poetry anthology)

Giro a vuoto (texts of songs)

Aeschylus, *L'Orestiade* (translation)

Travels around Third World countries with Alberto Moravia and Elsa Morante

Launches out on his own as a film author and director

His first film, *Accattone,* is a success at the Venice Biennale

Accused of seducing minors, though mostly without legal consequence

La religione del mio tempo (poems)

Scrittori della realtà dal VIII al XIX secolo (anthology)

Accattone (screenplay and film)

Films *La ricotta;* first meets the fourteen-year-old Calabrese peasant boy Ninetto Davoli, with whom he begins a passionate friendship and affair; they collaborate on almost all of his subsequent films

Il Sogno di una cosa | Dream of Something (novel)

L'Odore dell'India | The Scent of India (travel writings)

Mamma Roma (screenplay and film)

La ricotta | Let's Have a Brainwash (film, premieres 1963)

Lengthy legal proceedings follow the premiere of *La ricotta,* ending in a blasphemy verdict and confiscation of the film

Begins work on his novel *La Divina Mimesis* (published 1975), Pasolini's version of Dante's *Divine Comedy*

Moves to Via Eufrate in the EUR *(Esposizione Universale Roma)* district

La rabbia (film)

Comizi d'amore | Love Meetings (film, premieres 1964)

Il padre selvaggio | The Savage Father (screenplay)

Plautus, Il vantone (translation)

1958

Angelo Roncalli is elected Pope John XXIII ("Pastor Paganus")

1959

Cuban Revolution

Maria Callas ends her stage career (as Medea in Cherubini's opera) at Covent Garden, London

1960

Labor troubles begin at Fiat and other Italian factories; many last until the mid-1970s

1961

Yuri Gagarin is first man in space

Assassination of Patrice Lumumba, leader of the Congolese independence movement and outspoken critic of colonialism in Africa

Construction of the Berlin Wall

The Cold War reaches its peak

1962

End of the war in Algeria (1954–1962)

Death of Marilyn Monroe

USSR and USA carry out nuclear tests

Second Vatican Council (to 1965)

1963

Death of Pope John XXIII.

Assassination of John F. Kennedy

Martin Luther King, Jr. delivers his "I Have a Dream" speech at the March on Washington for Jobs and Freedom

Films *Il Vangelo secondo Matteo* in Matera, southern Italy, which later in the year wins an *Office Catholique International du Cinéma* prize at the Venice Film Festival

His essay *Nuove questioni linguistiche* is the first to confront the cultural decline of Italy

Poesie in forma di rosa (poems)

Sopraluoghi in Palestina (film, premieres 1965)

Il Vangelo secondo Matteo | The Gospel According to St. Matthew (screenplay and film)

Lectures on *La mimesi dello sguardo* in Pesaro; makes Roland Barthes's acquaintance

Films *Uccellacci e uccellini* near Rome, collaborating with the famous comic Totò

Poesie dimenticate (poems)

Alì dagli occhi azzurri | Ali Blue Eyes (prose)

Potentissima signora (songs and dialogues for Laura Betti)

Uccellacci e uccellini | Hawks and Sparrows (screenplay and film, premiere 1966)

Pasolini and Alberto Moravia take over as editors of the literary magazine *Nuovi Argomenti*

Convalesces from a stomach ulcer, during which time he writes plays

First visit to New York

Looks for a possible location in Morocco to film *Edipo re*

Totò dies

Develops an interest in Greek tragedy as a subject for films

La terra vista dalla luna (film, premieres 1967)

Films *Edipo re* in northern Italy and Morocco

Lettere agli amici 1941–1945 (letters, published 1976)

Che cosa sono le nuvole? (film, premieres 1968)

Edipo re (screenplay and film, premieres at the Venice Biennale)

Publishes attack on the student movement in *L'Espresso* (polemical poem *Il PCI ai giovani!!*)

Begins writing weekly column called *Il caos in Tempo* magazine

Premiere of *Teorema* at the Venice Biennale; the film banned by the Vatican on the grounds of obscenity, but the ban is later revoked

Teorema (novel, screenplay and film)

La sequenza del fiore di carta (film, premieres 1969)

Appunti di viaggio per un film sull'India (television production)

Orgia (play)

Films *Medea* in Turkey, Tuscany, and the Laguna di Grado

Becomes friends with Maria Callas

Pasolini on Pasolini (interviews)

Porcile | Pigsty (film)

Appunti per un'Orestiade africana (film, premiere 1973)

Medea (film, premiere 1970)

Medea drawings

Patmos (poem)

1964

1965

1966

1967

1968

1969

Krushchev deposed

Beginning of the Vietnam War (lasts until 1973)

Death of Palmiro Togliatti, co-founder and general secretary of the PCI (Italian Communist Party)

Racial unrest in the USA

Student ferment

Alexander Dubček's attempt to introduce socialism with a human face (the "Prague Spring") in Czechoslovakia is suppressed by the invading Soviet army

Death of Ho Chi Minh

Founding of the "Lotta Continua" revolutionary student group

Following a series of attacks earlier in the year, a bomb attack on the Banca Nazionale dell'Agricoltura, Piazza Fontana, Milan, leaves sixteen people dead

American Neil Armstrong walks on the moon

Pasolini and Sergio Citti write the screenplay for Citti's *Ostia*

Trip to Africa with Alberto Moravia, Dacia Maraini, and Maria Callas

Purchases the tower of Chia, near Viterbo, which becomes his place of retreat

Begins work on the novel *Petrolio* (published 1992)

Films *Il Decameron* in Naples and surrounding area

Starts painting again

Poesie (poems)

Il Decameron (film, premiered in 1971)

Appunti per un romanzo dell'immondezza (television documentary)

Obscenity charges follow the premiere of *Il Decameron*

Publication of his last volume of poetry *Trasumanar e organizzar*

Films *I racconti di Canterbury* on location in England and in Rome

I racconti di Canterbury | Canterbury Tales (film, premiered in 1972 at the Berlin Film Festival)

Supports a film by the extra-parliamentary "Lotta Continua" group *(Dodici Dicembre)*

Empirismo eretico | Heretical Empiricism (essays)

Numerous articles in the major Italian dailies, including *Il Corriere della sera,* collected in *Scritti Corsari* (Corsair Pages) and *Lettere luterane* (Lutheran Letters, published 1976)

Switches publisher from Garzanti in Milan to Einaudi in Turin

His old friend Ninetto Davoli gets married

Filming of *Il fiore delle Mille e una notte* in Ethiopia, Persia, Nepal, and Yemen; the film is the third in the "Trilogy of Life" after *Il Decameron* and *I racconti di Canterbury*

Il fiore delle Mille e una notte | Arabian Nights (film, premiered in 1974)

Le mura di San'a (documentary film)

Calderón (drama)

Works on film projects *Porno-theo-kolossal* and *San Paolo,* both remaining unfinished (publication of fragment of *San Paolo,* in 1977)

Films *Salò o le 120 giornate di Sodoma* in Salò, Bologna, and in Rome at the Cinecittà studios

Disowns the "Trilogy of Life"

November 2: Pasolini's corpse is found near Ostia

Arrest of presumed murderer, seventeen-year-old Giuseppe ("Pino") Pelosi

November 5: buried in the cemetery at Casarsa

La nuova gioventù (poems, revised version of La meglio gioventù)

La Divina Mimesis | Divine Mimesis appears (novel, written 1963)

Scritti corsari | Corsair Pages (collection of essays)

Salò o le 120 giornate di Sodoma | Salò, or the 120 Days of Sodom (film, premieres November 22)

1970 1971 1972 1973 1974 1975

The PCI (headed by Enrico Berlinguer) becomes the strongest and politically most influential Communist party in the West

First attack on the Italian government by the "Brigate Rosse" (Red Brigades) as judge Mario Sossi is kidnapped

P.P.P.

PIER PAOLO PASOLINI

Pier Paolo Pasolini and Death

Edited by
Bernhart Schwenk and Michael Semff
with the collaboration of Giuseppe Zigaina
Texts by Roberto Chiesi, Peter Kammerer, Loris Lepri,
Benjamin Meyer-Krahmer, Marc Weis, et al.

Pinakothek der Moderne, Munich

HATJE
CANTZ

Contents

Introduction

Thirty years ago on the morning of November 2, 1975—All Soul's Day—world-renowned director and author, Pier Paolo Pasolini, was found murdered on a small soccer field, in Ostia, near Rome; he had been run over several times with his own car. The shocking picture of the crushed body was seen around the world. Pier Paolo Pasolini—or "P.P.P.," as he himself abbreviated his name—was fifty-three years old. The violent death of one of the then most prominent, but also controversial, intellectuals in Europe led to a great deal of discussion and wild speculation. Even today, the exact circumstances cannot be established beyond doubt.

In May 2005, the self-confessed murderer, Pino Pelosi, revised his official statement regarding the circumstances. The male prostitute, who was then a minor, had been sentenced in 1976 to nine years in prison. Today he claims that Pasolini was murdered by several men unknown to him, and that their threats compelled him to take responsibility for the murder and remain silent, out of fear for his own life and that of his family.

The investigation of Pasolini's death, soon to be reopened, is causing unrest in Italian legal circles. For the public prosecutor's office in Rome had not only been satisfied to let the case rest thirty years ago with an improbable-sounding confession, but it can also be proved that they blocked further investigations. When a jury came to the conclusion that several perpetrators had been involved, the public prosecutor's office immediately filed an appeal. For them, Pasolini was the victim of an altercation that was "typical of homosexuals."

Bernhart Schwenk
Michael Semff

Today, thirty years later, the public prosecutor must take this new state of affairs into account.

Pier Paolo Pasolini was a director, but also a playwright and actor, poet, theorist and journalist, painter and illustrator. As an eminent poet, he made use of the Friulian dialect of his home in his early work; as an author of novels *(The Ragazzi, Il sogno di una cosa)* and essays *(Scritti corsari, Lutheran Letters),* as the director of sensational films *(Accatone, Mamma Roma, Theorem, Medea,* and *Salò, or The 120 Days of Sodom*—premiered just days after his death), as well as an illustrator and painter, he focused in particular on timeless, archaic themes, such as religion, sexuality, death, and the fate of mankind. With an aesthetic of contradictions that was all his own, Pasolini always went beyond the norm and created pictures of a lucidity that has hardly been matched since and in which violence and tenderness are intertwined like siblings.

Pasolini aimed throughout his career at achieving the universal, the ideal. Thirty years after his death, his great perceptiveness and the influence of his creations on later generations involved in the fine and performing arts, has now become clearer. Pasolini was one of the first to foresee the crises of the human race in the late twentieth and early twenty-first centuries—in particular the destructive influence of media and mass consumerism on culture. Early on in his creative life, he developed techniques of language and imagery that allowed him to switch effortlessly between mediums.

From the beginning, Pasolini's visionary, provocative, and critical worldview, the complexity of his works, and his uncompromising nature met with misapprehensions and rejection, but at the same time furthered his international fame. Among the general public, one still associates Pasolini's name with superficial events, scandals, and a disregard for taboos. To this day, a more detailed analysis of his films and writings, of his prose and poetry—or of any number of his additional artistic activities—is still lacking. Thus, thirty years after Pasolini's death, it seems imperative to us that one of the most important European authors of the second half of the twentieth century be introduced, in a new and fundamental way, to a younger generation interested in his achievements.

The reception of Pasolini's works in Germany was most intense during the 1980s and 1990s. Not only was an abundance of secondary literature written in German, but more than three dozen of his works were translated into German (though most of these are now out of print). In addition, several exhibitions, including one at the Munich Kunstverein, in 1982, and another at the Berlin Academy of Arts, in 1994, have contributed to a better understanding of important aspects of the artist's work.

For the impetus to approach Pasolini's work anew, we would like to thank the Friulian painter, illustrator, and author Giuseppe Zigaina, whose lifelong artistic friendship with Pasolini began in 1946. Since as early as the 1950s, Zigaina has maintained active contacts within Germany, which became lasting bonds thanks to the high esteem in which he was held, in particular, by Werner Haftmann. In 2001, the Staatliche Graphische

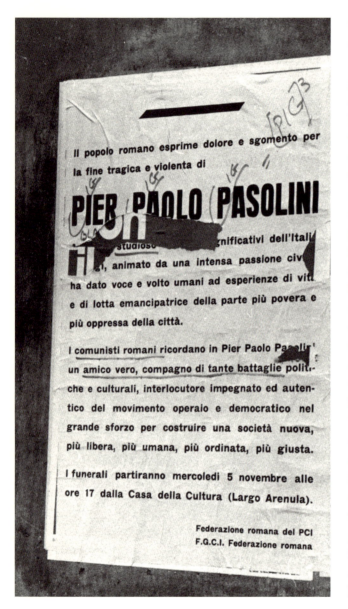

Il popolo romano esprime dolore e sgomento per
la fine tragica e violenta di

PIER PAOLO PASOLINI

studioso   nificativi dell'Ital
   , animato da una intensa passione civ
ha dato voce e volto umani ad esperienze di vit
e di lotta emancipatrice della parte più povera e
più oppressa della città.

I comunisti romani ricordano in Pier Paolo Pa   '
un amico vero, compagno di tante battaglie politi-
che e culturali, interlocutore impegnato ed auten-
tico del movimento operaio e democratico nel
grande sforzo per costruire una società nuova,
più libera, più umana, più ordinata, più giusta.

I funerali partiranno mercoledì 5 novembre alle
ore 17 dalla Casa della Cultura (Largo Arenula).

Federazione romana del PCI
F.G.C.I. Federazione romana

Obituary banns for the
Communist Party in Rome, 1975

Sammlung in Munich presented a retrospective of his drawings and etchings in the Neue Pinakothek.

For more than twenty-five years, Zigaina has occupied himself with deciphering a mythical and religious code that, in his eyes, imparts "compelling meaning" to Pasolini's oeuvre. In 1983, he published the article "Total Contamination in Pasolini," in the *Stanford Italian Review,* in which he interprets Pasolini's death as "one of the author's works"—as a "portrayal of 'mystery' that he not only predicted, but also arranged." This argument, which Zigaina has since expounded on in numerous publications, forms the backbone of our project and is laid out in detail in his essay. Zigaina sees in Pasolini the *ur* Christ, or modern gnostic, who feels obliged to bear witness to his "belief in reality and the effectiveness of myths." Peter Kammerer, a well-known expert on Pasolini's work for many decades now, contributes to this volume an enlightening discussion with Zigaina on his German translation of Pasolini's poem *Patmos* (1969). Our book has also been enriched considerably by Roberto Chiesi's informative essay on the motif of "the vision" in Pasolini's work, as well as by Loris Lepri's examination of Pasolini's observations on, and fierce criticisms of, cultural changes in Italian society. In turn, Benjamin Meyer-Krahmer investigates in his essay the technique of inter-media writing, which corresponds well with one of the chief goals of our exhibition: to present Pasolini explicitly as an artist who embraced a large number of different media in his works. Marc Weis contributes to our book his knowledge of the cultural historian Roberto Longhi, with whom Pasolini studied and whose "wonderful lectures" played an important role in the life of an artist who embraced film, poetry, prose, theory, painting, and drawing as equal partners in his creative work; Pasolini spoke fondly of Longhi's lectures time and again. To all of the authors who contributed to this book, we would like to express our most heartfelt thanks.

The exhibition represents the first extensive collaboration between two partner museums in Munich, the Staatliche Graphische Sammlung and the Bavarian Staatsgemäldesammlung, and hosted by the Pinakothek der Moderne, which has thus fulfilled its mission—to embrace a wide variety of genres in its presentations—in an exemplary fashion. Many institutions and individuals contributed to the success of the exhibition.

In particular, we owe thanks to Giuseppe Zigaina and his wife Maria for their untiring assistance and hospitality. The inspiring exchange of views and experiences, as well as their willingness to make precious loans and documents available to us, have proved to be indispensable to the project.

Other valuable loans, including drawings, manuscripts, and two painted self-portraits, were entrusted to us by the Gabinetto Scientifico Letterario G.P. Vieusseux in Florence. Here we must thank Gloria Manghetti and Maurizio Copedè for their openness and patience in solving various problems and accommodating us so kindly with regard to special loan requests. We especially need to thank the Centro Studi – Archivio Pier Paolo Pasolini in Bologna, which granted us generous access to its large collection of photography, which was

managed, until her death in July 2004, by Laura Betti, founder of the Pasolini Foundation. In Bologna, Roberto Chiesi, Loris Lepri, and Luigi Virgolin were particularly kind and helpful.

Finally, we feel exceedingly fortunate that it was possible for numerous documents and several drawings presented at an exhibition in the Círculo de Bellas Artes in Madrid—all loans from the Gabinetto Vieusseux in Florence—to be transferred directly to us. For this kind opportunity we give our thanks to the curator of the Madrid exhibition, Alessandro Ryker.

A second main pillar of the exhibition at the Pinakothek der Moderne can be found in the Munich Filmmuseum, which is offering an in-depth presentation of Pasolini's work as a film director. We warmly thank its director Stefan Drössler, as well as Klaus Volkmer, for the fruitful and extremely helpful collaboration.

During the many months of preparing for the exhibition in Munich, Angela Maria Opel and Carolin Angerbauer provided invaluable assistance with our biographical, bibliographic, and filmographic research. Last but not least, Ilaria Furno Weise from the Circolo Cento Fiori e.V. in Munich, with her dedication and friendly demeanor, helped establish important contacts and quickly solve any problems that happened to arise.

We are indebted to the following individuals for their suggestions and advice: Stefano Agosti, Corrado Albicocco, Cristina Benussi, Angela Biancofiore, Silvia Biancucci, Achille Bonito Oliva, Gianpiero Brunetta, Roberto Budassi, Carlo Alberto Buiatti, Giancarlo

Calidori, Adele Cambria, Daniele Capezzone, Miguel Angel Cuevas, Francesco De Majo, Patrizia De Michelis, Floriano De Santi, Enzo Di Martino, Jean Duflot, Thomas Feldkircher, Aris Karamaounas, Helga Leiprecht, Stefano Lorenzetto, Mladen Machiedo, Luigi und Patrizia Martini, Friederike Mayröcker, Andrej Medved, Fran-cesca Nesler, Marco Pannella, Ilario Quirino, Johannes Reiter, Klaudia Ruschkowski, Natasha Sarszovska, Christa Steinle, Francesca Valente, Marco Vallora, Peter Weibel, Peter Weiermair, and Zoltan Zubornijak.

Furthermore, without the help of a sponsor, this exhibition would have hardly become a reality. Our special thanks are due to Antonio, Fiorenzo, Gaspare, and Giancarlo Lucchetta of Gruppo Euromobil for their generous support of our project. Gruppo Euromobil per la Cultura has been sponsoring international art exhibitions for many years, and most importantly provided support for Giuseppe Zigaina's Pasolini research.

And, once again, the production of the accompanying German and English publications lay in the reliable hands of Hatje Cantz Verlag. Here, we must give our heartfelt thanks to the managing director Annette Kulenkampff for the dedication she showed to our project from the very outset. Furthermore, we would like to thank Eugenia Bell and Tas Skorupa for their editorial support.

For the design of this book, as well as that of the exhibit, we give our thanks to the Berlin design firm, chezweitz—and to Detlef Josef Weitz and Benjamin Meyer-Krahmer in particular. Together with their team and graphic designer, Rose Apple, they transformed our ideas and developed them even further with impressive creativity.

Our last thanks goes to Graziella Chiarcossi, Pier Paolo Pasolini's niece. We have her profound empathy for others to thank for the fact so many different individuals were able to work on this project in an atmosphere of such remarkable cooperation and harmony.

Bernhart Schwenk *is curator of contemporary art at the Pinakothek der Moderne in Munich.*

Michael Semff *is director of the Staatliche Graphische Sammlung in Munich.*

P.P.P.

PIER PAOLO PASOLINI

Poet
Pedagogue
Prophet

Preceding page
Pasolini in Grado, 1949

Pasolini and Death

A Purely Intellectual Thriller
Giuseppe Zigaina

I've never adequately considered why, from a certain point in my life, I felt an obligation to reconstruct the tragedy of Pasolini.

Perhaps it was because I found myself involved in one way or another, or more probably out of rage because I wanted to tear it from the literal interpretation which has disfigured that (apparently) incomprehensible "strophe of seventy times seven [thousand] violins and one large drum" the author talks of so sarcastically.

How and why Pasolini involved me in his story we shall perhaps discover in the course of rearranging a life ('s work) that—thirty years after his violent death—has already become mythic, despite being rooted in real life. It is a tale that the author served up with wholly unexpected means, as in the way he intimated to the audience in the prologue to *Affabulazione* that his tragedy "has an end but no beginning." What he didn't say there and then was that he was not talking about the play, the beginning of which he himself, the "shadow of Sophocles," was announcing from the stage, but about his own very private story as a man and an artist that would, as initially prophesied, would come to an end on All Souls Day, 1969.[1]

In this essay, I should like to relate as simply as possible that at the end of the 1950s Pasolini had resolved to express himself in a language[2] that was comprehensible to only a very few young people—a strategically constructed language with two or more levels of meaning. After the author's death, the reader could choose the one that allowed him to coordinate everything from the perspective that the author had determined for his massively autobiographical narrative, which was finally attested by a suicide, presented to the world as *Preghiera su commissione* (Prayer to Order), and also in these

lines dated March 1969: "I have a poetic notion of the grass. / And I know poetry's excess. / Which is why I have commissioned lines, / for my consecration (!) / ... to pray in this sacred space / (where, to tell the truth, I don't walk with bare feet)."[3]

The grass Pasolini talks about is that of the small football ground in Ostia where he "prayed" on the night of Sunday, November 2, 1975, and celebrated the myth of resurrection from death. He was thus following a ritual that he himself had ordered and described in advance: "By constantly making their presence felt, martyr directors [end] by their own choice when they finally get what they aggressively want: to be wounded and killed with the weapon that they themselves offer the enemy."[4]

The fact is that Pasolini, a "martyr director by choice," also prophesied when his expressive strategy would be understood as authentic and comprehensible—after he had fixed the year, the month, the day, and the order of events in the "cultural ritual" that would be celebrated in the *spazio sacro* in which he "would enter as Christ without taking off his shoes." "As long as I am not yet dead, no one can claim to really know me, i.e. make sense of my action, which is, linguistically considered, therefore difficult to 'decode.'"[5]

A reader who wants to unravel the "project and secret"[6] of Pasolini's death now, thirty years after it happened, cannot avoid testing the following three "working hypotheses." After comparing the consistency of the ascertained facts with each other, he can make his choice. The first two hypotheses have been

---

[1] Cf. Pier Paolo Pasolini, "Poesie mondane," *Le poesie* (Milan, 1975), p. 345. In *poesia mondana* (June 12, 1962) Pasolini discovers that he is forty, and prophesies: "And I / in arrears with death, before time / for true life, drink the nightmare / of light like a coruscating wine." He is a latecomer for whose death? If we take the

thirty-three years of Christ's life as a reference point, we discover that Pasolini is seven years "in arrears," and at the same time seven years "before time"—starting from June 12, 1962, the date he wrote the lines—in respect of his "true life," i.e life after death (1962 + 7 = 1969). The circumstances that confirm this (admittedly unique)

interpretation of Pasolini's announcement are numerous, including those compiled in the "Second Book" of *Trasumanar e organizzar* (Milan, 1971). Cf. also Giuseppe Zigaina, "Foreword," in idem., *Pasolini e il suo nuovo teatro "senza anteprime, né prime, né repliche"* (Venice, 2003).

[2] Cf. also the introductory words in *Una disperata vitalità*: "Record of the pre-history in the / 'discourse' of the current 'jargon': Fiumicino, the old castle and a / first true idea of death."

[3] Pier Paolo Pasolini, *Medea un film di Pier Paolo Pasolini* (Milan, 1970), p. 113.

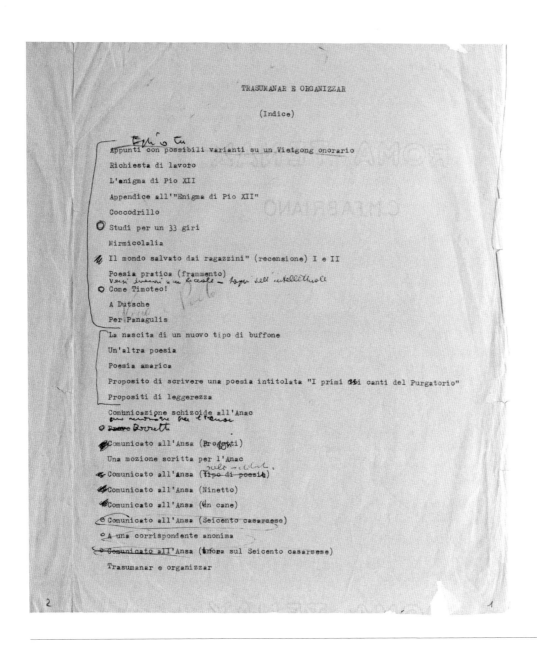

4 Pier Paolo Pasolini, "Cinema impopolare," *Nuovi Argomenti* 20 (October–December 1970); idem., *Heretical Empiricism,* trans. Ben Lawton and Louise Barnett (Bloomington, Indiana, 1988).

5 Pier Paolo Pasolini, "Osservazioni sul piano sequenza" (1967), *Empirismo eretico* (see note 4), p. 241.

6 Cf. Pier Paolo Pasolini, *Petrolio* (Turin, 1992), p. 182.

Contents page of *Trasumanar e organizzar,* 1971
Typescript with handwritten entries
Gabinetto Scientifico Letterario
G. P. Vieusseux, Florence

peddled by the mass media time and again, whereas the third—which I presented at the University of California Berkeley, in 1983—was published in the *Stanford Italian Review* under the title "Total Contamination in Pasolini."[7] Pasolini was a victim of any number of possible murders; Pasolini was assasinated by the secret services because of his attacks on the Christian Democratic government; Pasolini himself was the "organizer" of his own death, which, conceived as a form of expression, was intended to give meaning to his entire oeuvre.

Indeed, in following Mircea Eliade, James Frazer, and Ernesto de Martino—the ethnologists the poet/ film director used to consult—I landed in the middle of a thriller, looking for a solution. The plot can only be understood if you piece together logically the clues

scattered by the author—parts of a discourse that would make sense with a sacrificial death, as the following "permanent self-admonition" attests: "To be either immortal and without expression or express oneself and die."[8]

Apart from this "elementary proposition with a truth function,"[9] I should like to add something else that, as far as I know, no one has ever spoken about. Ever since the poem *La reazione stilistica* (The Stylistic Reaction) of 1960, Pasolini had—as someone who considered himself an alchemist—always treated the fundamental rule of alchemy, that of secrecy, with respect. But in this case, he could do so only partially, because he had first to thematicize the function of his death and then prophesy it liturgically, as was required by the representation of a myth. To be "one, but doubled," as he wrote in *La Nuova Gioventù* (The New Youth), he was accordingly compelled to express himself in a language that allowed him to linger in a strategic ambiguity.

But why did he express himself in an almost incomprehensible language? That is precisely the riddle that can only be solved by an attempt to understand the fear, the horror, or the indefinable, almost erotic pleasure that the poet felt in "organizing" his immolation—with existential, cultural, and religious objectives that had never been dreamed up before by anyone. It was as if a latter-day saint not recognized by the Catholic church sought martyrdom as a renunciation of mortal life that would at the same time be a passing over to life after death—perhaps to be understood as the artist's presence in human memory. But to answer the ques-

---

Pasolini with Giuseppe Zigaina in Grado, 1969

[7] Giuseppe Zigaina, "Total Contamination in Pasolini," in: *Stanford Italian Review* (Stanford, 1984).

[8] There is a variant of this postulate in the following remark of Pasolini's that is also a declaration: "Thence the reason for death. If we were immortal we would be immoral because our example would never come to an end, hence it would be indecipherable, eternally suspended and ambiguous." Cf. Pier Paolo Pasolini, "Living Signs and Dead Poets," *Heretical Empiricism* (see note 4). There is another version in "Is Being Natural?," also in *Heretical Empiricism*.

[9] This is a formulation (from Wittgenstein's *Tractatus logico-philosophicus*), which because of its verbal essence can only be related to a real fact.

tion that many people ask in respect of this "case," I would say that Pasolini's fear, which he suppressed with the painkiller Optalidon, was due to uncertainty over whether he would be capable of bringing his "death project" to completion. He might, for example, be prevented by cancer, as he wrote in the *Progetto di opere future* (Project of Future Works), or by a fatal car accident—if not by the stomach ulcer that became steadily more painful. Failure would have made him a "timid, romantic admirer of death." That is why Pasolini, in the expectation of being able to celebrate the creation myth he longed for, had to announce it to the world with ambiguous "linguistic games" inspired by the theories of Freud and Wittgenstein. They are passionate games for a "few thousand young people scattered in the ghettos of the big cities," but always ambivalent, as is seemly in the shadow of *thanatos*. As ambiguous as these verses in his *Progetto di opere future:* "One must disappoint. Only a noble drivel / of mixed inspirations, demystifies / if miraculously chaos leads to solid clarity … / which codifies reality in full"; "In this 'story' … I shall disdain every preceding arrangement and, under the precursive / sign of Marx and the one that follows, / of Freud, I shall re-establish new hierarchies in the realm / of poetic loves: and with my humble wit / will counter literary existence / with the notion of Unexpressed Existent, without / which everything remains a mystery."

In order to decode it, one should note that the transition from chaos to the cosmos is the manifestation of the original cosmogonic creation myth. The "myth of resurrection from death" that Pasolini celebrated in Ostia is a creation myth at an artistic and expressive level. Our author thus "made poetry" with his death, also in order to "establish new hierarchies in the realm of his poetic loves." In this way he asserts that literary existence (which permits an artist to remain alive after death) is precisely the opposite of the earthly existence of a poet (one of many), who lives but in no way knows how to express himself because he was born to be an "unexpressed existent."[10]

Only now, having given a few examples of Pasolini's language, can I make the reader "who laughs not, who loves and enthuses," familiar with the first part of the "introductory remark" to *Scritti corsari* (Corsair Pages), in which the author asks a reader of just this kind to reconstruct for himself the "scattered and incomplete work" of a poet who is on the verge of dying. And as we see, that is a religious repetition, like the symbolic "closing of the circle" that the author ventured on with *La nuova gioventù,* in 1974. As far as language is concerned, I shall only add that the word "book," as appears at the beginning of the above "introductory remark" acts as *pars pro toto* for the life's work in its entirety. It says there: "The reconstruction of this book is left to the reader. He has to assemble the fragments of a scattered and incomplete work. He has to put together various pieces that nonetheless complement each other. He has to arrange the contradictory elements and discover their essential unity. He has to eliminate possible inconsistencies (i.e. abandoned investigations or hypotheses). He has to replace the repetitions with possible variants (or take the repetitions as passionate anaphora)."[11]

---

[10] Cf. Pier Paolo Pasolini, "Progetto di opere future," *Le Poesie* (see note 1), p. 525.

[11] Pier Paolo Pasolini, *Scritti corsari.*

It follows from this that the really enthusiastic reader must first find the formulae with which Pasolini communicates his death project to the world; he then has to free them from their linguistic context, which puts them in a frame of reference in some way. Finally he has to arrange them chronologically in order to reconstruct the logic of a "narrative" that is in this case timeless. If the reader then succeeds in finding the two or three variants that the author raised for his prophetic announcements (the "course corrections," including the postponement of his planned death from 1969 to 1975),[12] he will need to keep them in order, to adjust them at a technical, expressive level. In other words, if the reader does not succeed in intuitively recognizing that Pasolini strategically encrypted his language from the end of the 1950s, he will never be able to fit the discourse together as a coherent, logical system. We need always to bear in mind the fundamental assurance: "Death lies not in not being able to communicate but in no longer being understood."[13]

I remember often going to the nearby basilica in Aquileia at the end of the war to play a game reconstructing the "myth of Jonah." It was a story that, with its many poetic allusions to Gnostic motifs, spread across the broad floor of the church, had long been known and familiar to me, almost as a part of my own life experience. Only over the years did I become aware that the peculiar feeling of "experiencing" something came from the fish in the mosaic. They were so "scientifically" depicted in the prophet's story, as if they were there to demonstrate their presence not only in the mosaic, but also in the re-

ality of my life. One after the other, I identified them by their species. They were the fish I dreamed of catching in the Gulf of Trieste. In the cool stillness of a Gnostic basilica, Pasolini, whom I took there in 1949, certainly cannot have thought that his Jonah would symbolically anticipate his story as a poet who manipulated "three" words of Dante's to celebrate his own "myth of resurrection from death," which means, let's say it without hesitation, representing the myth of Pasolini in accordance with the myth of Jonah, as relived by the Finnish hero Väinämöinen. Like the latter, he too was a "poet, singer, and builder of boats"[14]—those new means of communication.

But since today anyone talking of the improbable is regarded with suspicion, it could be that Pasolini, as an "early Christian or modern Gnostic," felt obliged to bear furious witness to his "faith in the reality and effectiveness of the myth." His faith was like that of an early Christian who still believed in the Kabbala, in magic, the transubstantiation of alchemy, and thus the reality of the host consecrated by the Word as the true flesh of Christ. And this was only a surface contradiction in a poet and film director who defined himself as a Marxist, Communist, and heretical empiricist all at once, since he (realistically) believed in the effectiveness of myth, or rather in the opportunity that this would offer him of introducing a further level of meaning into his own diverse language.

If we follow this trail, we could reconstruct the story of a Friulian woman's son born in a village called Casarsa, on the River Delizia. Roland Barthes—who, if

---

[12] Pier Paolo Pasolini, "Progetto di opere future," *Le Poesie* (see note 1).

[13] See note 1.

[14] Cf. Mircea Eliade, *History of Religious Ideas,* vol. III (Chicago, 1988). "In the *Kalevala*, the Finnish national epic that Elias Lönnrot compiled (first published in 1832), the main character Väinämöinen is 'eternally wise.' Of supernatural origin, Väinämöinen is an ecstatic visionary endowed with numerous magical capabilities. He is also a singer and harpist."

Pasolini as Giotto in
the *Decameron*, 1970

he had had time to read Pasolini, would have immediately grasped his expressive strategy—had, with his
gift of anticipation, already postulated that "a mythical
narrative is a thriller of the intellect." So much so that
Pasolini, who described his own tragedy as a "purely
intellectual thriller,"[15] not only repeated the French linguist's illuminating remark, but bore witness to it "with
his body and his blood"—even though "neither Plato
nor Aristotle had taken into account the possibility of
a discourse lived out."[16] And that is perhaps the reason
why I am retelling the story of a friend who was found
dead on a football pitch in the grey light of dawn on
Sunday, November 2, 1975, with his face so disfigured
that only after repeated examination did it become clear
that it was not a "pile of rubbish" (as someone said) but
the massacred body of Pier Paolo Pasolini.

At that time, as an extremist taboo-breaking poet,
film director, and unrelenting castigator of the Social-
ist-Christian Democratic government, who in his turn
was accused variously of "causing public nuisance," was
the Italian intellectual most often in the headlines. We
should bear in mind that his last film, *Salò o le 120 giornate di Sodoma* (Salo, or the 120 Days of Sodom; 1975),
contained a concealed announcement of his forthcoming violent death. He had long previously compared the
function of editing the miles of material filmed during
the work on a film with the effect that death has on the
infinitely many "acts" that a person carries out in his
earthly life. These, once recognized as "essential and
significant," are removed from time by death. In *Empirismo eretico* (Heretical Empiricism) he says:

"Death makes a brilliant montage of our lives, i.e. it sin-
gles out the really significant ... moments and places
them in a sequence. It thus turns our infinite, unstable
and uncertain, and therefore linguistically indescrib-
able present into a clear, stable and therefore linguistically (i.e. within the framework of a General Semiology) precisely describable past."[17]

A few hours before his death, Pasolini sent me a
"linguistically precisely describable" message to announce that the "editing of his last film" was complete.
The news—which at that point I did not recognize as
such—was formulated neither in writing nor speech,
but consisted of the original rolls of film for *Salò, o le
120 giornate di Sodoma* in six metal cans, which someone had left at the entrance to my house in Cervignano
during the night of November 5/6, 1975. The same
evening I called my friend Guido Botteri, who at the
time was the editor-in-chief of RAI (Radiotelevisione
Italiana), in Trieste, to ask him for advice. Botteri immediately sent someone to collect the film, and got it
screened at the Capella Underground club there. I was
also asked about the film by the Salone Pier Lombardi
(now the Teatro Franco Parenti) in Milan and later had
it delivered to the director there. On the evening of November 8, 1975, *Salò o le 120 giornate di Sodoma* was
confiscated by the judiciary after a screening in Milan,
and a discussion about censorship in Italy followed (in
which Piero Ottone, Carlo Ripa di Meana, Gioivanni
Testori, and judge Pulitano took part).

At this point it makes sense to give visitors at the
Pinakothek der Moderne in Munich, for an exhibition

---

[15] Pier Paolo Pasolini, "Frammento
IV: Praga," appendix to *Bestia
da Stile, Pier Paolo Pasolini Teatro*
(Milan, 1988).

[16] Pier Paolo Pasolini, "La ricerca
del relativo," *Medea un film di
Pier Paolo Pasolini* (Milan, 1970).

[17] Cf. Pier Paolo Pasolini, "Osservazioni sul piano sequenza" (1967), in
Heretical Empiricism (see note 4).

commemorating the thirtieth anniversary of Pasolini's death, a few essential facts about the author's life work. An author because of his declared "belief in the effectiveness of myth" was celebrating the "myth of resurrection from death" with his violent death, on an aesthetic, linguistic, and religious level. And this was after he had announced his death to the world as a "cultural ritual," in his *Manifesto per un nuovo teatro* (Manifesto for a New Theatre) in 1968, which was designated by him as the conclusion of his "diachronic work." The facts in it must be considered from the viewpoint of their chronological development. The few remarks about Pasolini that I now add could contribute to the materialisation of a "thriller of the intellect," which, after the thirty years in which it has been spoken of, seems to interest a "few thousand young people, scattered in the ghettos of the cities." A thriller, moreover, whose solution was clearly presented by the author to be read as a "victory over the urge for self-preservation, which is at the same time is a linguistic-semiological violation." In this way, its (mystic) relevance seems more and more palpable, even as its "new theatre without pre-performances, premieres, or repetitions" becomes a text more and more difficult to understand. The visitor in Munich should therefore know the following: Pasolini—born in 1922, in Bologna, to an elementary school teacher and professional officer— spent the years of World War II in the birth place of his mother Susanna—a village between the Alps and the sea called Casarsa, or Casarsa della Delizia in full, which means "place of burnt-down houses (i.e. repeatedly

Still from *Mamma Roma,* 1962

The finding of Pasolini's body in
Ostia, November 2, 1975

burnt down by the Turks) by the River Delight." This latter incongruous topographical term became to the young poet a symbol of a "desperate vitality" to which the aroma of eroticism always clung. In this indefinable aura, it happened that Pasolini's brother Guido, three years younger than him, was killed by a group of Communist guerillas who were working with Tito's 9th Corps. Pier Paolo, who had remained with his mother in Casarsa "to fight with the weapons of poetry," thereupon joined the Italian Communist Party. When he was suspended from teaching two years later on a charge of "seducing a minor" and kicked out of the Party, the local uproar was so great that the writer was forced to "flee to Rome, like in a novel." And there, a long way from Friuli, the life he lived on the god-awful fringes of the Italian capital was desperate indeed. But happy, too—so he would later say—as it gave him a chance to discover "a great Baroque, Catholic, and spacious city."

In 1957, he published *Le ceneri di Gramsci* (Gramsci's Ashes), a collection of poems that prompted Alberto Moravia to speak of the author as a "grande poeta civile (great civilized poet)," though the term may not have pleased Pasolini. But *Ragazzi di vita* and *Una vita violente,* the two novels in which Pasolini used the terse argot of the Roman suburbs, again brought him into conflict with the law, and on the same charge—"causing a public nuisance." The Christian Democratic press isolated him, the Fascist press sneered at him as a "dirty homosexual," and the Roman Communists, who knew nothing as yet of his exclusion from the party, termed him an "irresponsible populist." With the onset of the

decline in the great Marxist utopia, the literary avant-garde felt it could accuse him of being only a "nostalgic poet of the peasant world of the nineteenth century." Pasolini swallowed his fury and responded with a film, *La ricotta:* "I'm only a force of the past … [but also] more modern than any modernist." Effectively, this meant he already had in mind the vision of something that would be the second objective of his life—that "raging, [reluctant] [or dying]" life. Indeed he said—in the *La nuova gioventù*—that when he was "really living the spring" he had planted the "flowers of passion," whereas after he had planted "the flower of the game" spring "had given him none of its heavenly days."[18] This was a game in which the author, who gambled everything on the game of "fame and life from eternity to eternity," had decided to leave the world for good, initially set for

---

The coat of arms of Casarsa
della Delizia

[18] Cf. Pier Paolo Pasolini, variant of "La seconda forma de *La meglio gioventù." La nuova gioventù* (Turin, 1975), p. 163f. From mid-1968, Pasolini constantly thought of killing himself in April. But after closely re-reading Mircea Eliade's *Myth and Reality,* he came to the conclusion that the "myth should be celebrated at night, between

autumn and winter, on a holy day." After that, in order to be the first to intensify the significance of this date, he organized his death for the night of November 2, All Souls Day, that fell on a Sunday in the perpetual calendar (indeed a religious day). The days that met all the criteria were All Souls Day of 1969 and 1975.

1969, and then pushed back to 1975. Not in defeat, but as a victor over every kind of "self-preservation." Partly as a challenge to his detractors: they themselves would have to solve the secret of a self-proclaimed "film director martyr" who "wants to be wounded and killed with the weapon that he himself aggressively offers to the enemy." A project that Pasolini had already offered to the world, in the "alternative of desire and holiness," whereby he was making use of Freudian projection, allowing himself, in a general silence, the following aphorism: "In dying, Kennedy expressed himself through his last action."[19]

This aphorism sarcastically requires the name Kennedy to be replaced by the name Pasolini. In this way, the true structure of a Freudian projection—"in dying, Pasolini expressed himself through his last action"—can be seen as a formula reduced to its smallest verbal denominator, summarizing an artist's life, work, and objective of a sacrificial death; an artist who wanted to express himself in dying in a scandalously existential-linguistic-religious project—defined by him as "plurilingual molasses or a monolithic cord";[20] an author who ultimately did not wish to be a poet or playwright, writer, director, or painter, but only a "force of the past, more modern than any modernist." It was an objective he had already alluded to in the poem *La reazione stilistica* in 1960: "They deceive themselves, monsters, that death / is a leveler! They do not know that it is in fact death / (its alibi as Catholic servants), / that breaks up, corrodes, mangles, distinguishes: / also language. / Death is not order, haughty / monopolists

of death, / its silence is a language too diverse / for all you to make use of: / around precisely this revolves / life."[21]

In these words, Pasolini tells us that the "silence of death" (his death), not death in general, is a language that enables him to "express himself at the highest level." An assertion that he reinforces with this aphorism: "A saint also speaks in silence, with his body and his blood." With the prophetic lines of his *Reazione Stilistica*, the poet referred his reader to the following things: Death is not a general leveler, but creates differences, judgments, real and truthful cultural and linguistic divisions; to be understood, the cryptic language he expresses himself in needs to be supplemented "what will be and is not yet"—i.e. his celebration of the myth of the resurrection of death in Ostia; what revolved around his death in 1960 was not mortal life but his life after death.

It is a fact that 1960 is the year Pasolini quit literature—"but never poetry"—to devote himself almost entirely to the cinema; he made *Accattone* and then *Mamma Roma*. In 1964, he made *Il Vangelo secondo Matteo* (The Gospel According to St. Matthew) with his mother Susanna in the role of the Virgin (who burst into tears beneath the Cross when the director said that the crucified victim up there could be her son). He made this film in order to announce his future *imitatio Christi* to the world—through film, the "language written by reality." He did not say thereby that he would attest to his death with the spoken language of reality, i.e. with his "extreme action."

---

[19] Cf. Pier Paolo Pasolini, "Osservazioni sul piano sequenza" (1967), *Heretical Empiricism* (see note 4).

[20] Cf. note 10.

[21] Pier Paolo Pasolini, "La reazione stilistica," in "La religione del mio tempo," *Le Poesie* (see note 1).

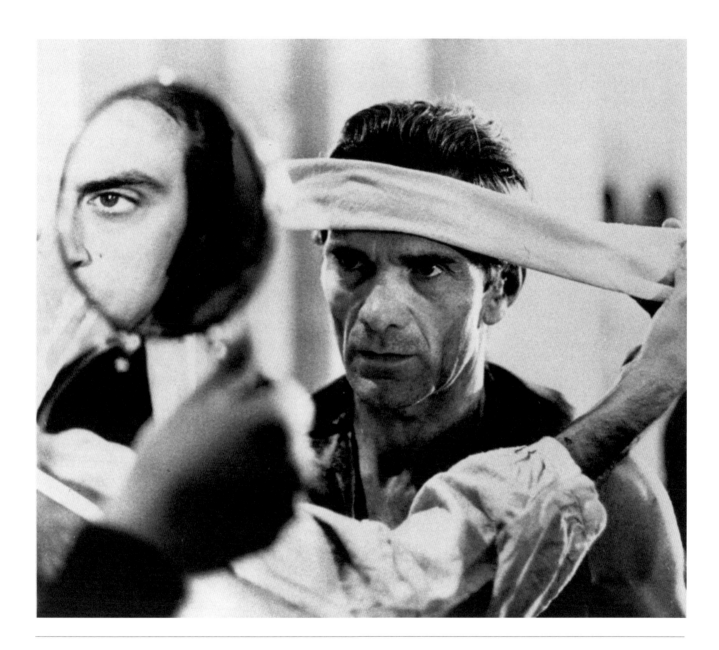

Pasolini as Giotto in
The Decameron, 1970

The cinema had to solve three existential problems for Pasolini:

1. He had to express himself in a trans-national language comprehensible to everyone.

2. He wanted to "manifest his presence in the world" by means of the *amplificatio* that Jung equates with the gesture of the alchemist, who fans the fire beneath the crucible in order to obtain the elixir of life.

3. He had to use the vocabulary of film in order to be able to speak of himself in an ambiguous fashion.

In this way, the poet succeeded in further elaborating his "project of a mystery" until he arrived at a solution, which, as he wrote, "would place his life in the centuries." In other words: his invention on a linguistic level was so new "that every already proven idea seemed to be overtaken by something new." Roland Barthes had demanded that semiology should be "cautious" because "this knowledge must be capable of being used, at least projectively, on non-linguistic objects." Pasolini—who broke taboos in unimaginable ways—made the great French linguist's prophecy come true in order to be able to define himself as "an experimental rabbit, not a human being any more."[22]

[22] Roland Barthes, *Elements of Semiology,* (New York, 1977).

Giuseppe Zigaina *is a painter, draftsman, graphic designer, and writer. He became a friend of Pier Paolo Pasolini in 1946.*

The author would like to thank Carlo Alberto Buiatti for his support and Ilario Quirino for his research on perpetual calendars.

P.P.P.

PIER PAOLO PASOLINI

Preacher
Pioneer
Philosopher

Preceding page

Pasolini filming *Medea*, 1969

The Chosen Image

Pasolini's Aesthetic of the Drawn-Out Moment
Bernhart Schwenk

In the beginning of the film *Il Vangelo secondo Matteo* (The Gospel According to St. Matthew), there is a long silence. For eight seconds, the eye of the camera rests on the face of a young woman. She looks at another person with uncertainty, almost fear.

The second shot shows the face of a man. His face, too, is helpless, clouded over, not entirely free of an expression of reproach. The third shot repeats the close-up of the woman, who now casts her eyes downward and slowly lowers her head. The fourth lets us look for another eight seconds at the man's face. Not until the fifth shot is the very pregnant woman shown in full against a walled-off arched window, and in the sixth shot appears the whole figure of the man as well. All but motionless and silent, yet at the same time rich in suggestive power, this sequence of living stills tells the story of a relationship. The persons shown, and there is no doubt despite the absence of words, are the Virgin Mary and Joseph of Nazareth. The heartfelt yet deeply uncertain married relationship of these simple people is palpable. Only at the end of this first film sequence does music cautiously begin, and the camera follows Joseph as he leaves the house.

The principle described above, that of the silent succession of unmoving single images in varied form, recurs multiple times in the film. The exchange of looks between Mary and Joseph after the Annunciation seems like an echo of the evocative opening sequence. Now her troubled expression dissolves into a soft, hopeful smile. Soon thereafter, the camera focuses in a similar fashion on the Magi, the Pharisees, and the soldiers killing the children of Bethlehem. In these highly static scenes, the camera fixes on the heads of the men, one after another, as the same detail of a picture, in the same close-up view. The viewer reads arrogance and self-satisfaction in the silent faces closed off like masks, recognizes hope

and the wisdom of age in the furrowed expressions of the old people, and is confronted with the faces of the peasant youths, which reflect a readiness for violence and a raw sensuality. Pasolini also shows the naming of the disciples in close-up, through single images. The impressive portraits of these men are at once an expression of different ages and an illustration of difference in human physiognomy; they insist above all on expressing typologies, as the prior shots did, and make exemplary reference to the unalterable existence of an archaic social structure.

The precisely composed images of motionlessness and of silence are a characteristic motif of Pasolini's filmic handwriting. In particular the close-up must be described as all but a trademark of his cinematographic gaze. We note the paradoxes of this conspicuous preference of Pasolini's, and will seek to make clear why the artist chose a halted temporality for the originally dynamic medium of film.

The slow, silent pans dispense with drama of any kind. They almost seem like documentary footage seeking to abandon all illusion. And yet these are concentrated shots of great intensity. They are simple, timeless images, particularly distinguished by their limitation to the essential. They seem familiar to the spectator; they are called up like déjà-vus of a collective visual memory. They carry with them far more than their function as elements of a well-known narration, the events of the Bible; they should be understood instead as areas open to interpretation, comparable to the abstraction of words or the ambiguous character of holy scripture. It

The twelve apostles in stills
from *The Gospel According to*
St. Matthew, 1964

is about "representation, not action, incorporation, not plot, motionlessness, not flow."[1]

With *Gospel,* shot in 1964, Pasolini succeeded in creating a work that was compelling because of its religious (which is to say, timeless) theme. Yet the film's award at the Venice Biennale did not come without misunderstandings. After all, the director's first film, *Accatone* (1961), was harshly criticized precisely for this aesthetic of the stationary (which manifested itself not only in individual images, but also in the story as a whole). The "eternal" images Pasolini created, set to classical music, were read as a metaphor for the unalterable hopelessness of a social class, the sub-proletariat. This provoked leftists in particular, who strove to change and improve social conditions. In this way, it was inevitable that Pasolini would become a social outsider. As a communist, he sympathized with the dispossessed and underprivileged of this world. He belonged on the other hand to an intellectual upper class, which he nonetheless rejected as misguided and decadent. In a time when the dynamic of progress was valued above all, and when thinking in contradictions was still unusual, Pasolini's aesthetic of the stationary could only be rejected as anti-modern.

Pasolini's contradictory understanding of film as a moving medium for the demonstration of the static is also on display in his representation of landscape and architecture. In his second film, *Mamma Roma,* the city plays the role of a leitmotiv. The view of a contemporary residential district appears several times like a modern *veduta,* appearing, like a heavenly Jerusalem of the pe-

tite bourgeoisie, as a symbol of a better, more carefree life. This panorama-like still is more than an ordinary "establishing shot"; it has the effect of a dreamlike spell. The direct, frozen view of modern residential blocks in the open country, on which the ruins of an ancient aqueduct bear witness to another epoch in history, illustrates a visible present into which the past and a melancholy anticipation of the future are melted together. This image of the city appears again like a *fata morgana* at the close of the film, after the death of young Ettore. For *Mamma Roma,* once held up by her son's future, it has become an unreachable illusion full of bitterness. This isolated still of condensed time enters into the viewer's consciousness and, as a condensed story, unleashes emotions.

In 1964, seeing the triumph of Pasolini's *Gospel,* Andy Warhol demonstrated, with *Empire,* his own extreme idea of stopped or slowed time. Whereas Pasolini sought symbolism in his tableaux, Warhol aimed, in his eight-hour-long, "boring" filming of the Empire State Building, directly at making the importance of the building, deeply anchored in American national pride, fade away.[2] Both artists were nonetheless equally interested in the conscious subversion of the medium of film, which corresponds to the process of vision, and so enabled reflections on the images themselves precisely through motionlessness.

For Pasolini, this gaze held in place should never stiffen, which would kill off the tension and devalue the image. He thus always makes a conscious decision to write fragility and ephemerality into the motionless

[1] Birgit Jooss, "Die Erstarrung des Körpers zum Tableau. Lebende Bilder in Performances," in: ed. Christian Janecke, *Performance und Bild. Performance als Bild* (Berlin 2004), p. 272. See also ibid., "Das nicht enden wollende Bild. Der Aspekt der Dauer innerhalb von Performances," in: eds. Karin Gludovatz and Martin Peschken, *Momente im Prozess. Zeitlichkeit künstlerischer Produktion* (Berlin, 2004), pp. 113ff.

[2] See Ulrich Wilmes, "Die Erinnerung an das Morgen," in: *Geschichten des Augenblicks. Über Narration und Langsamkeit,* exh. cat. Städtische Galerie im Lenbachhaus, Munich (Ostfildern-Ruit, 1999), pp. 113f.

moment as well. The urban *veduta* unites the new and the old, the modern with the legacy of the ruins. In the faces, a smile reveals a gap in the teeth or reveals a look of youthful uncertainty. Pasolini never fixes on a look of stable ideality, but rather the moment of beauty in the coincidental and the unconscious. It is the irregularities of the individual that create the desired atmospheric, sensual, lively space for association.

The connection of this contemplation (the camera), the spell of the individual, meaningful image, to Pasolini's particular interest in visual art, and in Italian Renaissance and Mannerist painting in particular, is attested elsewhere.[3] Significant in this regard is the subject of his art history thesis, which went missing in the turmoil of the World War II: Giorgio Morandi, the master of the still life, whom Pasolini often credited as being one of his idols. His "great fondness for Bonnard," for the painter's "afternoons full of quiet and sun over the Mediterranean," also provides insight into Pasolini's understanding of images.[4] Likewise, the representations of frontal views of (individual) figures or vessels in his drawings demonstrate his interest in the limitation of the visual and in an idea of the image crystallizing an eternally valid time.

The propensity for contemplation and for motionlessness and the concentration of action in an image are evident in Pasolini's writings as well. In his early novel *Il sogno di una cosa* (The Dream of a Soul; 1962), Pasolini denies himself the continuous textual development of plot or drama. When he does describe events (a political

---

Pasolini filming *The Gospel According to St. Matthew,* with Enrique Irazoqui as Jesus, 1964

3 See, e.g., Günter Minas, "Ein Fresko auf einer grossen Wand. Die Bedeutung der Malerei für die Filmarbeit Pasolinis," in: ed. Christoph Klimke, *Kraft der Vergangenheit. Zu Motiven der Filme von Pier Paolo Pasolini* (Frankfurt am Main, 1988), pp. 51ff. See also the article by Marc Weis in this catalogue, pp. 53–64.

4 Pier Paolo Pasolini, notes in the literary bequest, circa 1970, German translation in: eds. Johannes Reiter and Giuseppe Zigaina, *Pier Paolo Pasolini. Zeichnungen und Gemälde* (Basel, 1982), p. 8.

meeting, young people at a fair, women in the kitchen in the evening, etc.) in detail, he hardly ever mentions the contents of conversations. Much more important to him are certain moods, the representation of an atmosphere. Pasolini thus recalls, in one of his essays, his quest in his early poems to find "well-chosen words for a style *sublimis*."[5] These "well-chosen" words should be understood as poetic images, as the examples named in the essay just mentioned, "wild vegetables, nightingale" illustrate with the senses. Pasolini's remarks on the poet Sandro Penna, whom he revered, are also enlightening in this regard. They make clear his interest, in poetry, in letting "the mystery and the absoluteness—the purity—of things, from which they take their inspiration, continue to exist," which indeed reflects Pasolini's own conception. Pasolini speaks of "moments in which time, filled up, purifies itself and overflows into the absolute," of "moments of richness in which is prophesied the mystery which is not understood," and lastly of "stoppages, the *intermittences du cœur* in which the gesture, because it is so wonderfully integrated into the anonymous body of the day, would have been all but overlooked and stands out, isolated, in a kind aureole of consciousness."[6] The blink of an eye, the moment, the halting, the isolated—all of this attests to Pasolini's aesthetic consciousness for the single image.

In 1961, with *Accatone*, film became a means for Pasolini to set in motion an inner world of images developed over the course of two decades. Yet it was to remain, for the whole of Pasolini's life, a motion conceived in stills, in direct confrontation like a still life,

"a world made up of many individual poses."[7] Pasolini believed in timeless images that predated or existed outside of language, in images of myth and ritual. Only in such images might be preserved the individuality and humanity which Pasolini saw threatened—before the age of globalization—by technology and the influence of mass media.

In contrast to the Neorealists, in particular Vittorio De Sica (1902–1974) and Roberto Rossellini (1906–1977), Pasolini never sought fidelity to the truth, but rather a stylization of reality, its aestheticization. It is therefore no wonder that in *La ricotta*, for example, identifiable paintings from art history are recreated in detail. "One can see *La ricotta* as a collage. The film's painterly passages are quotations which have a highly precise function: to quote the two Mannerist painters Rosso Fiorentino and Pontormo. I have recreated their pictures in detail. Not because they share my point of

[5] Pier Paolo Pasolini, in: *L' Illustrazione Italiana* 89 (January 1962).

[6] Pier Paolo Pasolini, in: *Il popolo di Roma* (September 28, 1950).

[7] Achille Bonito Oliva, "Pier Paolo Pasolini und die Tradition des italienischen Manierismus," in: Reiter/ Zigaina 1982 (see note 4), p. 12.

Photographic specification for a camera position in *The Gospel According to St. Matthew*, 1964 view or because I love them—it is not about my representation in the first person—but rather just to show the inner state of the protagonist, a director conceiving a film about the Passion. This conception is the exact opposite of the one I had used before to make *Il Vangelo*. The quotations also have something exorcistic about them: They are reconstructions of extreme precision, sophistication and formality: precisely what I did not want to do in *Il Vangelo*, and what I therefore foisted polemically onto the character of the director. Not that I have something against directors of Bible films; it was not a polemic against bad taste, but rather against an excess of good taste."[8] Pasolini's much-discussed *tableaux vivants*[9] after the model of identifiable paintings may thus be understood as an artistic banter, polemic formulations against perfection, and a warning against that which is all too cultivated.

This aesthetic conception appears to radicalize in Pasolini's later films. The images now follow a still stricter choreography, growing more artificial, at times more exalted and more despairing. Yet Pasolini was fascinated to the last by the moment captured and expanded by the camera, by thinking in framed single images. In *Edipo re* (Oedipus Rex; 1967), the camera remains for fifty seconds—a very long period of time in a film—on the face of a silent Silvana Mangano, and in her face are joy and sorrow, obsession, and estrangement. In *Salò o Le 120 giornate di Sodoma* (Salò, or The 120 Days of Sodom; 1975), the faces are no longer lively and warm, as they were in *The Gospel*. Instead, the faces of the sadistic upper-class, merciless and cold, are intercut with the

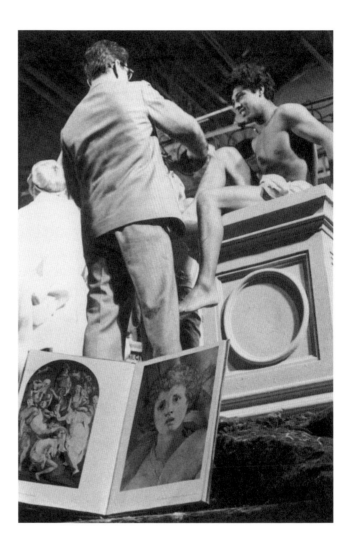

8 Pier Paolo Pasolini, quoted in: eds. Franca Faldini and Goffredo Fofi, *L'aventurosa storia del cinema italiano: ranccontata dai suoi protagonisti 1935–1959* (Milan, 1969).

9 See, e.g., Sabine Folie and Michael Glasmeier, *Tableaux Vivants, Lebende Bilder und Attitüden in Fotografie, Film und Video,* exh. cat. Kunsthalle Wien (Vienna, 2002), pp. 46ff.

Pasolini filming *La ricotta*, 1962, with a book of paintings by Pontormo in the foreround faces of the young people who are being held prisoner. The "well-chosen" images are the subject of a cruel aesthetic test arrangement. The taunting or fear-filled face becomes the mirror of a harried soul. Everything is now in a pale light. The carefully constructed group shots are arranged in stage-like spaces in which the spectator is situated in the middle of the actors. In contrast to the older generation, particularly Luchino Visconti (1906–1976), with his nostalgically voluptuous, extravagant interiors, there is in Pasolini the nightmarish atmosphere of a suppressed uproar. Here there is no more hopeful longing for a valid reality. This is a resigned, indeed cynical, representation via eccentric means outside the norm. More than ever before, Pasolini is interested, in his last film, in transforming inner states into poses. The path leads inevitably from the jolly rural wedding table, at which Mamma Roma amuses the party with young pigs, to the decadent "communion" in Salò's villa at which steaming excrement is served up in a silver dish. There seems to be no way out of this alchemy of the frozen image. The tortures that follow are observed, like picture puzzles, only through the "fixed frame" of a window onto the courtyard. The spectator is almost grateful to see the dance of two boys, and with it a slowing of time, a moment of consolation that holds off the lethal catastrophe—at least as long as the music plays.

On November 3, 1975, a vivid image blazed across the cover pages of the Italian daily papers, an image all but uncannily linked to Pasolini's aesthetic of stopped time. The image shows Pasolini's own slaughtered body, covered by a tarpaulin and lying on the sandy ground,

surrounded by police, press, and rubberneckers. As though Pasolini had known how the mass media would pick up this image, distribute it, and inject it into the collective visual memory of the public, he lay there—like "a piece of garbage," as the woman who found his body said. This silent tableau, archaically graphic, was like one of the bodies that died in agony before the dusty gates of Thebes in *Edipo re,* and also like *Accatone,* the protagonist of Pasolini's very first film, who himself lay in the street dying. A symbolic still life presents a human as what he always has been: a vulnerable piece of matter. But the deep emotion that could be unleashed by such "well-chosen" images may have been the single and last hope that Pasolini still carried.

Still from *La ricotta* based on
Pontormo's *Deposition,* 1963

Bernhart Schwenk *is curator of contemporary art
at the Pinakothek der Moderne in Munich.*

Still from *The Decameron,* 1970

P.P.P.

PIER PAOLO PASOLINI

Polemical
Paradigmatic
Promiscuous

Slide Show Inspiration

On the Effect of Roberto Longhi's
Interpretation of Art on Pasolini
Marc Weis

Ingmar Bergman got the bug when he first went to the movies as a child: "It was the beginning for me. I caught a fever, and since then it's never let me go."[1] Luis Buñuel was infected when he saw a film by Fritz Lang: "When I saw *Der müde Tod*, I sensed with utter certainty that I wanted to make films."[2] And Pasolini?

He seems to have caught the film bug, or the bug for directing films, not in a cinema, but rather through Roberto Longhi's art history slide lectures.

The films of Pier Paolo Pasolini have, indeed, often been linked to painting.[3] The grounds for this are—above all—his striking compositions that quote paintings.[4] In his film *Il Decameron* (The Decameron; 1970), the director programmatically takes on the role of the genius painter Giotto. He expands this role beyond Boccaccio's original, displaying his own partiality for painting, and for that of the early Renaissance in particular, and its exemplary role in his early film works: "What I have as a vision in my head, in my field of vision, are the frescoes of Masaccio and Giotto … I can understand no paintings, landscapes, or compositions of figures which have no link to this, my early passion for the painting of the fourteenth century, which has man as the center of every representation."[5]

There are, nonetheless, in all only a few clear quotations from paintings, and most of these function to contrast or satirize.[6] For Pasolini, there seems to exist far more complex connections to the visual arts. His reaction to critics' reductionistic interpretation of the death sequence in *Mamma Roma* (1962) provides a clear point of reference here: "Ah Longhi, step in, explain that it is not enough to show a foreshortened figure with feet in the foreground to speak of the influence of Mantegna. Do the critics have no eyes? … Or could one perhaps speak, if at all, of an absurd, superior mix of Masaccio and Caravaggio?"[7]

Pasolini also dedicated *Mamma Roma* to the man who lectured him in art history (at the University of Bologna between 1939 and 1943) with the words: "for Roberto Longhi, whom I thank for my 'figurative inspiration.'"[8] Now he called on Longhi as a judge of interpretation. In fact, Pasolini's set-up corresponded to Longhi's view, according to which borrowed quotations are fruitless, and do not get at the essence of the model. In this way, Longhi criticized some purported successors of Masaccio's: "Quotations, in other words, always quotations and not representations in Masaccio's sense, even then, in the fourth decade of the [fifteenth] century. And always fabulous, unreal, abstract revocations of these new and so concrete facts."[9]

In the aforementioned closing scene of his second feature film, Pasolini did have Mantegna's *Lamentation* in mind, but following film syntax, he created a montage of shots for the group of figures in the painting. In *Mamma Roma*, the weeping mother is first placed "alongside" the dying son through parallel cutting: For the moviegoers the two are optically and psychologically connected, though within the film narrative they are kept apart by prison walls.

Pasolini makes reference to Caravaggio and Masaccio as representatives of realistic-existential forms of representation. He feels a fundamental obligation to their use of light, including chiaroscuro, and to their simple and yet magnificent compositions of figures. The technique of his first four films, which Pasolini attributed to "figurative culture," is accordingly simple, almost barren.[10] He preferred to work with non-professional actors. The shots were often filmed without

---

[1] Ingmar Bergman, *My Life in Film* (London, 1994).

[2] Luis Buñuel, *My Last Sigh* (New York, 1984).

[3] See in particular: Giuseppe Zigaina, *Pasolini und der Tod. Mythos, Alchemie und Semantik des glänzenden Nichts* (Munich, 1989).

[4] Main examples may be found in the films *Mamma Roma* (1962; Leonardo and Ghirlandaio/Mantegna), *La ricotta* (1962; Pontormo/Rosso Fiorentino), *Teorema* (1968; Francis Bacon/Warhol), *Il Decameron* (1970; Giotto), *I racconti di Canterbury* (1971; Bosch/Brueghel).

[5] Giuliano Briganti, "Aveva negli occhi Giotto e Pontormo," in: *La Repubblica,* July 1989, p. 25.

[6] For example, the colorful Mannerist tableaux vivants in *La ricotta* (1962), which the director in the film—played by Orson Welles—rehearses according to models from Rosso Fiorentino and Pontormo.

See also the text by Bernhart Schwenk in this book, pp. 41–49.

[7] Pier Paolo Pasolini, *Le belle bandiere. Dialoghi 1960–65* (Rome, 1977), pp. 230f.

[8] Pasolini's 1974 essay on the occasion of an edition of Longhi's works is the most extensive testament

sound (a soundtrack was added later). The result is a large arsenal of faces available to Pasolini for his imagined images. Filming was done on coarse-grained, contrasty Ferrania P.30 film stock, which was also used for Italian newsreels. Little camera movement, first usually with a normal lens, then more and more telephoto, so as to transmit figures, compacter yet, onto the screen. Filming was almost always done in daylight, most often with limited back-lighting and heightened contrasts: "[The technique] used expressed itself stylistically in barrenness and severity. The elementary has become absolute: precisely what I sought when I transferred the figurative model of Masaccio to the cinema."[11]

The film *Il Vangelo secondo Matteo* (The Gospel According to St. Matthew; 1964) offers a more in-depth examination of Pasolini's self-reflexive connections to art, and to art history. By using the text of the New Testament, "the plot of which everyone knows," the director is able to "unambiguously give visual expressive force precedence over plot."[12] Pasolini himself demands a stylistic way of reading.[13] In this film, too, he makes reference to his highly complex appropriations from painting, to the influences of Giotto and of Piero della Francesca.[14]

Il Vangelo secondo Matteo is constructed in four parts. The two brief, almost wordless parts are the symmetrical beginning and end of the film: Birth / Youth and Condemnation and Death / Resurrection. The main theme of the two long middle segments are the sermons and preaching of the advancing Christ. The film is characterized, down to the compositions of fig-

ures, by the recurring search for a regular, symmetric order. In the disputation between Jesus and Caiaphas, for example, two groups of people are planimetrically and paratactically constituted, linked to the center. This closed form of representation, which is markedly present in religious paintings of the Renaissance, is the result of endurance, often with a peculiar festiveness and obedience to a higher law.[15]

Many motionless close-ups of faces make reference to the three-quarter portraits popular in the closing years of the Quattrocento.[16] Pasolini quite consciously modelled the pregnant Virgin Mary on Piero della Francesca's paintings in Sansepolcro and Monterchi. In this image, he sought the unity of "royal" and "popular," simple character.[17] In doing so, he appears to directly

---

to this relationship: P.P. Pasolini, "Roberto Longhi, Da Cimabue a Morandi," in: ibid., *Descrizioni di descrizioni* (Turin, 1976), pp. 251–255. In a still unpublished text on the occasion of Longhi's death, Pasolini wrote: "The culture revealed and symbolized by the Maestro opened up an alternative to all reality previously known."

From the literary archive with Graziella Chiarcossi. I thank Laura Betti for making me aware of this central document.

9 Roberto Longhi, "Fatti di Masolino e di Masaccio" (1940), in: Longhi, *Da Cimabue a Moranti. Saggi di storia della pittura italiana* (Milan, 1973), p. 324.

10 Oswald Stack, *Pasolini on Pasolini* (London, 1969), pp. 99. Pasolini already considered his fifth film *Uccellacci e uccellini* (Hawks and Sparrows; 1965) to be part of "cinematographic" culture.

11 Nico Naldini, *Pier Paolo Pasolini* (Berlin, 1991), p. 208.

Still from *The Gospel According to St. Matthew*, 1964

adapt the view of Longhi, who himself had years earlier described the *Madonna del Parto* in Monterchi as an "extremely simple, yet sublime representation."[18]

Another film scene inspired by Piero della Francesca is the baptism of Christ. Particularly noticeable is the borrowing of the similarly clothed Pharisees passing by in the background. Yet the camera movement into the rocky ravine, directly against the flow of the stream, and the long, silent, frontal close-up of the face of Jesus may be traced back to Piero's fashioning of the baptism, as may be the midday light and the spatial divisions as well. Three rustic youths, in lieu of Piero's three angels, stand out at the left of the baptism scene, and below them the two later disciples John and Jacob. Reading Roberto Longhi on Piero's painting makes the replacement of the heavenly beings with simple youths in the film unsurprising. Longhi describes the angels as specimens of newborn humanity similar to Masaccio's newborn humanity, only "less educated and more amazed," and as a "race sublimely peasantlike, but not rough, … angelic youths, come to earth like oak trunks, with thick ankles that in a few years will be unshakeable."[19]

Longhi describes the total composition in Piero's painting as a "sublime reconciliation, seemingly derived from the perfection of distances made in the right proportions, a perfection seamlessly connecting figure and landscape, near and far in the clear festiveness of the zenithal light." Here "all things have equal rights in their occupation of the freely assembled spaces," and "no longer have their value individually, but rather in

Stills from *the Gospel According to St. Matthew,* 1964

[12] Eric Rohmer takes this thesis, which may be applied to Pasolini's film, as the basis for his image-specific interpretations of Friedrich Wilhelm Murnau's *Faust;* Eric Rohmer, *Murnaus Faustfilm, Analyse und szenisches Protokoll* (Munich and Vienna, 1980), p. 9.

[13] Naldini 1991 (see note 11), p. 248.

[14] Jean Duflot, ed., *Pier Paolo Pasolini, Il sogno del centauro* (Rome, 1983), p. 115.

[15] See Heinrich Wölfflin, *Kunstgeschichtliche Grundbegriffe* (of 1915), (Basel and Stuttgart, 1984), pp. 147 f.

the totality reproduced in divine fashion by the perspectival eye."[20]

The "right proportions" in the "totality," the "reconciliation" invoked by Longhi, are also Pasolini's goals in ordering the course of the film. Pasolini took inspiration from the manifold connections, cross-references, doublings, and grammatical repetitions of his literary source, the Gospel of Matthew.[21] The network of links that characterizes *Il Vangelo secondo Matteo* does not faithfully follow the source material, however; Pasolini instead creates an ordering system of his own, primarily visually oriented. Amidst the wealth of references within the film, the phenomenon of similarly edited pairs of scenes is particularly unusual.

The path of Jesus to Nazareth is clearly shown to be formally parallel to the path taken by Joseph at the start of the film. Both scenes are assembled from nearly identical shots in the same order. The appearance of Jesus is, to be sure, emphasized more strongly: The pan across the city on the arrival of Joseph in Nazareth transitions into a shot of children at play, overseen by a larger boy. Then there appears an angel. In the later scene, the same pan ends abruptly to show Jesus, who from this place sends forth his disciples. In the linked context, Jesus thus allegorically takes on both the task of the watchful boy and that of the angel of the Annunciation.

Similar means are used to link other scenes—usually in pairs—to one another. The latter scene generally proves to be, following a typology, the heightening or fulfillment of the prior occasion. The phenomenon of clearly related scenes has its predecessors in fresco

[16] See also the text by Bernhart Schwenk in this book, pp. 41–49.

[17] Pier Paolo Pasolini, *Il Vangelo secondo Matteo* (Milan, 1964), p. 42.

[18] Longhi 1973 (see note 9), pp. 423f.

[19] Ibid., p. 371.

[20] Ibid., pp. 372f.

[21] See Pier Paolo Pasolini, *Il Vangelo secondo Matteo* (see note 17), pp. 16f.

cycles of the fourteenth century, and in Giotto as well. There, too, "shots" are repeated when nearly identical scenery of landscapes or architecture, for example, reappears at different events.[22] The binding architectural form can be understood as a sort of orientation system from which the differentiation between the scenes may more clearly be read. The identical succession of cuts in the pairing of scenes plays a similar function.[23]

Anticipation and intensification are also to be found in certain paintings of Giotto's, for example in *Christ's Entry into Jerusalem,* in Padua. The disciple at the left edge of the painting shows clear formal parallels to Jesus, who is riding ahead. If the painting is read in the usual direction, from left to right, the disciple can be understood as a more modest anticipation of the coming Christ. In Pasolini's version, the motif of the arrival in Jerusalem is announced twice at once. The entry of the three kings into the same city is shown through the same montage in the first part of the film. Analogously, an unknown horseman may be seen on this path shortly before the triumphal scene with Jesus.

The consistency between the depictions of Giotto and Pasolini extends from iconographical to compositional details, like the successive expansion of the coats in front of Jesus. More important, however, is the fundamental statement which the art historical literature has seen—as in Longhi's interpretation of Piero della Francesca—illustrated in Giotto's fresco compositions, and which Pasolini emulated through corresponding representational means: "Giotto's painting shows, expressed in a glimpse of the present-day, the entry of

Christ into Jerusalem as an event of inevitable necessity in the history of salvation."[24]

In the context of Giotto's universal order, each element has structural, and thus the same essential, value. One may speak of a unity of action, "of which the individual moments are only a part, but wherein they have their value."[25] Following this, the set-junctured structuring of *Il Vangelo secondo Matteo* should be read as a metaphor for an ordered understanding of the world. Here the depiction of a historical or psychological event is left out in favor of the inevitable character of the proceedings.[26]

On the other hand, *Il Vangelo secondo Matteo* is also marked by altogether different stylistic elements. The broken, moving hand-held camera images at the start of the bearing of the cross are one example. They are the result of Pasolini's resolve, in this film, to partially break through the "sacral photographic technique" worked out in *Accattone* (1961), since he found that the constant doubling of this "reverent" style seemed "ridiculous" with the sacral theme.[27] The search for closeness to the truth is clear in the portrayal of specific details, which the spectator notices as though by accident. A soldier collides with Jesus; another lets him drink. One sees the strain of raising the cross, the physical exhaustion of Christ, the boredom of the soldiers.

According to the screenplay, the scene of the condemnation of Christ is to start out in a way fundamentally like "one of a thousand episodes from 'colonialist' barracks."[28] At the Crucifixion, emphasis is to be placed on the "unbelievable physicality of pain."[29] In describing

---

[22] The "summary of those two scenes" in Giotto's Arena Chapel is treated more extensively in: Rudolf Kuhn, *Mittelalterliche Freskenzyklen 1300–1500* (Munich, 1984), pp. 230–232.

[23] The basis for this is the formation of dramatic unities in Pasolini, a formation corresponding to the distinguishing narrative style of Giotto: The Padua fresco cycle is made up of formally through-composed, independent constructions, even though all the paintings also exist in a common narrative context.

[24] Max Imdahl, *Giottos Arenafresken* (Munich, 1980), p. 65.

[25] Kuhn 1984 (see note 22), p. 210.

[26] One year after the completion of *Il Vangelo,* Pasolini named "style as the true protagonist" of the new cinema. He saw characteristics in Antonioni's *Deserto rosso* (The Red Desert; 1964) astoundingly similar to those shown by him in his own films: "The technique of letting the figures enter into the shot, which makes the montage, in sometimes obsessive fashion, into a series of 'paintings' [quadri]—which we can call informal—where the figures enter, do or say something, and exit once again, leaving the image once more to its pure, absolute signification as image; on this follows

4

Tutto ciò che io posso sapere intorno al Caravaggio è ciò che ne ha detto Longhi

E' vero che il Caravaggio è stato un grande inventore, e quindi una grande realista. Ma che cosa ha inventato il Caravaggio? Nel rispondere a questa domanda che non mi pongo per pura retorica, non posso che attenermi a Roberto Longhi. Il Caravaggio ha inventato: primo: un nuovo mondo che secondo la terminologia cinematografica si dice profilmico, intendendo con questo tutto ciò che sta davanti alla macchina da presa: il Caravaggio cioè ha inventato tutto un mondo da mettere davanti al cavalletto nel suo studio: tipi nuovi di persone, nel senso sociale e caratteriologico, tipi nuovi di oggetti, tipi nuovi di paesaggio. Secondo: ha inventato una nuova luce: al lume universale del Rinascimento platonico ha sostituito una luce quotidiana e drammatica. Sina i nuovi tipi di persone e di cose che il nuovo tipo di luce, il Caravaggio li ha inventati perchè li ha visti nella realtà. Si è accorto che intorno a lui – esclusi dall'ideologia culturale vigente da circa due secoli – c'erano uomini che non erano mai apparsi nelle grandi pale o negli affreschi, e c'erano ore del giorno, forme di illuminazione labili ma assolute, che non erano mai stati riprodotti e respinti sempre più lontano dall'uso e dalla norma, avevano finito col divenire scandalose, e quindi rimosse. Tanto che probabilme,te i pittori, e in genere gli uomini, fino al Caravaggio probabilmente non le vedevano nemmeno.
La terza cosa che ha inventato il Caravaggio è un diaframma (anch'esso luminoso, ma di una luminosità artificiale che appartiene solo alla pittura e non alla realtà) che divide sia lui, l'autore, sia noi, gli spettatori, dai suoi personaggi, dalle sue nature morte, dai suoi paesaggi. Questo diaframma, che trasponde le cose dipinte dal Caravaggio in un universo separato, in un certo senso morto, almeno rispetto alla vita e al realismo con cui quelle cose erano state percepite e dipinte, è stato stupendamente spiegato da Roberto Longhi con la supposizione che il Caravaggio dipingesse guardando le sue figure riflesse in uno specchio. Tali figure erano perciò quelle che il Caravaggio aveva realisticamente scelto, negletti garzoni di fruttivendolo, donne del popolo mai prese in considerazione ecc., e inoltre esse erano immerse in quella luce reale di un'ora quotidiana concreta, con tutto il suo suole e tutta la sua ombra: eppure... eppure dentro lo specchio tutto ciò pare come sospeso come a un eccesso di verità, a un eccesso di evidenza, che lo fa sembrare morto.
Posso amare criticamente la scelta realistica del Caravaggio nel ritagliare nei personaggi e begli oggetti il mondo da dipingere; posso amare, ancor più, criticamente, l'invenzio-

another similar image, into which figures enter, etc., etc. So that the world presents itself as though ordered by a myth of pure painterly beauty into which figures may penetrate, to be sure, but by adapting themselves to the rules of the myth's beauty, rather than desecrating it by their presence." Pier Paolo Pasolini, "La mimesi dello sguardo," in: Lino Miccichè, ed., *Per una nuova critica* (Venice, 1989), pp. 17–36, here p. 29.

[27] Stack 1969 (see note 10), pp. 83f.

[28] Pier Paolo Pasolini, *Il Vangelo secondo Matteo* (see note 17), p. 246.

[29] Ibid., p. 250.

"Tutto ciò che io posso saper intorno al Caravaggio è ciò che ne ha detto Longhi." (Everything I can know about Caravaggio is what Longhi told me), "La Luce del Caravaggio," from: *Descrizioni di descrizioni*, typescript, 1974

Still from *The Decameron*, 1972,
based on paintings by Pieter
Bruegel the Elder

Caravaggio's *Crucifixion of Saint Peter*, Longhi points out a similar kind of realism in art: "The painter observes the event like a detached cameraman, and the gestures of the workers are painstaking, though not those of the executioners, who have need to be cruel."[30]

In addition, certain shots in the film fall out of the strictly structured frame, shots termed in the screenplay as *"scene realistiche"* (realistic scenes). Pasolini sometimes sketches them in a few words: "a bunch of trees in the barrenness … rogues and splendor … goats and camels … in one corner, under old, crumbled stonework, a group of boys enjoying themselves, … some playing music."[31] These representations are not directly related to the main action. In his programmatic text "La mimesi dello sguardo," Pasolini makes a principle out of this tendency:

"Such a persistence in details, in particular details of excursus, is a digression from the context of the film: It signifies the temptation to make another film. It is, in short, the presence of the author, who in an abnormal freedom exceeds his film and continuously threatens to throw off the film for the sake of the desire of a sudden inspiration, which is the latent inspiration of the love for the poetic world of the individual's own life experiences."[32]

Roberto Longhi seeks to convey in his lectures an analogous fascination for dramatic details in painting. Today, this may also be understood with particular immediacy through his short film *Carpaccio* (1948),[33] assembled entirely from overall and detail shots of paintings by the eponymous Renaissance painter. In this artistic reality, the camera moves freely like an observer's curious eye and picks out details in the background, with zooms and cuts providing the transitions between detail and overall picture, as in a feature film. One must imagine Longhi's slide lectures to have been similar, the lectures which awoke Pasolini's enthusiasm and which he compared to a "fantastical critical film," in which Longhi contrasted an exemplary "shot of the world of a Masaccio in physical, material fashion against one of the Masolinian world, … in that constancy that is precisely so typical of the cinema."[34]

The parallels between Longhi's picture presentations and Pasolini's work on film become clearer yet when Pasolini says of himself: "If my pictures are in movement for a reason, it is because the lens moves across them as across a painting; I always conceive the background as the background of a painting … So the film camera moves across backgrounds and figures which

---

[30] Roberto Longhi, *Caravaggio* (Dresden, 1968), p. 44.

[31] Pier Paolo Pasolini, *Il Vangelo secondo Matteo* (see note 17), p. 117.

[32] Pier Paolo Pasolini, *Kino der Poesie* (see note 26), p. 69.

[33] In 1960, Roberto Longhi's *Carpaccio* (directed by Umberto Barbaro, 1948) was broadcast by the Italian television network RAI. Since the film was long thought to have been lost, it has not been considered in the literature to date. In 1988, Paola Scremin succeeded in finding *Carpaccio* again. I am grateful to her for making the film available to me for my research. It is the view of Laura Betti that Pasolini was also familiar with the film (conversation of November 18, 1990).

[34] Pier Paolo Pasolini, "Roberto Longhi. Da Cimabue a Moranti," in: *Descrizioni di descrizioni* (see note 8), p. 252.

Portraits of Roberto Longhi
Charcoal and pencil on paper,
each 48 x 36 cm
Gabinetto Scientifico Letterario
G. P. Vieusseux, Florence

are essentially received as motionless and dipped deep in chiaroscuro."[35]

In *Carpaccio,* the scenes are enlivened with Baroque music, and Longhi's commenting voice accompanies them continuously. The essayistic descriptions have the character of imagining the paintings in the present. With verbs and temporal clauses in the present tense, and by naming temporal or even climatic or acoustical (!) phenomena, they resolutely support the immediacy of the scenes and make possible a perception of them as realistic: "The trumpeters practice the new march on the step below: a group of persons that has come out of the fortress gates is decorated with the first rays of the sun, a troop of blacks makes ready a ship … " The discussion is of "daily life" as it plays out "between the light and shadow of the square." One sees the "unbelievable uniforms, from the headgear to the coats … and the … fashion fool with the luxurious hat on his blond mane." The relationship to the descriptions of the *scene realistiche* in Pasolini's screenplay is obvious.

Carpaccio vividly transmits Roberto Longhi's interest in endowing the imagistic work of a past epoch with a direct, living effect for the modern observer. The search for conceptual equivalences to "translate the visual into language,"[36] and the literary character which results from this, are often named as decisive principles of Longhi's art historiography.

Pasolini seems to take the opposing path. In his writing on film theory, he determines the cinema to be the "natural semiotics of reality." It allows him "to maintain the connection to reality, a physical, fleshly, indeed sensual connection."[37] Here he seeks a representation of things by means of themselves, that is, the letting-speak of the world without the detour of developed human systems of symbols. Arte Povera would soon pursue similar ends. Pasolini hoped to win the "archaic power of eidetic suggestion"[38] from these ephemeral discoveries in the outside world.

For Pasolini and Longhi alike, for the artist and for his art history professor, these seemingly opposed tendencies collide in the fascination for "the experience of reality." Since Longhi traced this experience of reality with particular intensity among the artists of the Renaissance,[39] it cannot be surprising that Pasolini took up these artists. This is because it is precisely Giotto, Masaccio, Piero della Francesca and—as in the example film—*Carpaccio* who connect a new experience of realistic representability with a sublime sense for the "holiness" of the underlying creation. Pasolini seeks such a sense when he speaks of the "holiness" he finds when devoting himself to art as regression to reality: Cinema and art as such are "possibilities to get closer to life in its perfect form."[40] "When I make a film, I shift into the state of fascination with an object, a thing, a fact, a look, a landscape, as though it were an engine where the holy were just about to explode."[41]

A step forward from a realistic view to a transcendental experience. A similar fraternal joining took place in the age of Masaccio, when painting on religious themes shifted to replace the "previous system of expression, the expressions and garments, with an infinitely rich fidelity to life."[42] Pasolini's wish seems to be to return

---

[35] Briganti 1989 (see note 5), p. 25.

[36] Andreas Beyer, "Roberto Longhi," in: Heinrich Dilly, ed., *Altmeister moderner Kunstgeschichte* (Berlin, 1990), p. 252.

[37] Pier Paolo Pasolini, *Il sogno del centauro* (see note 14), p. 29.

[38] Pier Paolo Pasolini, quoted in: Rolf Kloepfer, "Die natürliche Semiotik der Wirklichkeit. Ein Entwurf Pasolinis," in: Wetzel 1984 (see note 3), p. 83.

[39] When speaking of Longhi's descriptions of paintings, Pasolini himself emphasized Longhi's survey of "reality, which is presented in the paintings." Pier Paolo Pasolini, "Roberto Longhi, Da Cimabue a Morandi," in: *Descrizioni di descrizioni* (see note 8), p. 253.

[40] Pier Paolo Pasolini, quoted in: Rolf Kloepfer, "Die natürliche Semiotik der Wirklichkeit. Ein Entwurf Pasolinis," in: Wetzel 1984 (see note 3), p. 68.

[41] Pier Paolo Pasolini, *Il sogno del centauro* (see note 14), p. 121.

[42] Jacob Burckhardt, *Der Cicerone, Eine Anleitung zum Genuss der Kunstwerke Italiens* (Stuttgart, 1978).

Caravaggio, *Bacchus*, 1597 (detail)
Oil on canvas,
95 x 85cm
Uffizi, Florence

Ettore Garofalo as Ettore
in *Mamma Roma*, 1962

to this "newborn sensual beauty, which must have its unabridged share of the earthly and real,"[43] as Jacob Burckhardt formulated the awakening of the art of the Renaissance. Pasolini's affinity for the spiritual outlook of the aforementioned painters should thus be understood first and foremost as an affinity for Longhi's view, and this thus clarifies and resolves the paradox that a director pursues, by his own admission, a natural semiotics, that is to say direct recourse to the real world of objects, yet has in his films a wealth of correspondences and links to the culture of a past epoch. Determining the influence of early modern painting on Pasolini may thus be done precisely by establishing that the influence is one mediated through Longhi's art historical observation.

An example may once again briefly illustrate the peculiar transfer: In 1961, Pasolini met a young waiter in a tavern in Rome who, in Pasolini's view, carried a basket of fruit in "the manner of a boy by Caravaggio."[44] It was Ettore Garofalo, who later appeared in *Mamma Roma* as, unsurprisingly, a somewhat careless waiter with a basket of fruit. Here Pasolini once again followed the concepts of his teacher, true almost down to the word. In Longhi, one may read, for example, a description of Caravaggio's *Bacchus* in the Uffizi: "There we have a lazy and sleepy worker in a Roman *osteria*, coincidentally crowned with grapes of all colors."[45]

Longhi tracks the concrete reality in Caravaggio's painting, Pasolini recognizes in reality the fascination of the painterly prototype and gives the experience new form in a (film) painting. It is ultimately unsurprising

[43] Ibid., p. 750.

[44] Stack 1969 (see note 10), p. 51.

[45] Longhi (1952), 1973 (see note 9), p. 815.

that, in the interrelations between this protagonist of art history and that protagonist of the cinema, Pasolini's basic filmic principle itself, that of making old art fruitful, seems already to have been present in Roberto Longhi. Of the coloristic expressive power of film, Longhi wrote in 1950: "Very true, that the most memorable passages of color film to date are those where the director has created most intensively out of the painterly culture that already exists."[46]

[46] Roberto Longhi, "Editoriale," in: *Paragone* 1, no. 3 (March 1950), pp. 4f.

This text is a revised version of the essay "Ah Longhi, greifen Sie ein! Pasolinis frühe Filme zwischen Realismus und Kunstinterpretation," in Giuseppe Zigaina and Christa Steinle, eds., *Pier Paolo Pasolini oder Die Grenzüberschreitung. Organizzar il trasumanar* (Venice, 1995).

Marc Weis *studied the history of art, with a special focus on film, in Munich and Karlsruhe. As an artist, he collaborates with Martin De Mattia under the name M + M.*

Preceding page
Pasolini with Maria Callas, filming
Medea, 1969

1 Still from *Accattone,* with Adele
Cambria as a young mother from
Sicily with her children, 1961

2 Still from *Teorema,* with Silvana
Mangano as the industrialist's wife
and mother of two adolescents, 1968

3 Pasolini, with his mother Susanna as
the Virgin Mary, during filming of *The
Gospel According to St. Matthew,* 1964

4 Pasolini with Margherita Caruso
as the young Virgin Mary
during filming of *The Gospel
According to St. Matthew,* 1964

Anna Magnani and Ettore Garofalo
as mother and son in *Mamma Roma*,
1962

1

2

3

1 Anna Magnani as Mamma Roma
  dancing at the wedding of her
  former pimp, 1962

2 Pasolini on the football pitch,
  1955

3 A scene from *Hawks and
  Sparrows*, outside the Las Vegas
  Bar, 1965

4 Dancing boys, in a scene from
  *Salò, or The 120 Days of
  Sodom*, 1975

4

1

2

3

1 Looking for a location on Etna, for *Teorema*, 1968

2 A still from *The Gospel According to St. Matthew*, filmed near Matera, in Basilicata, 1964

3 A scene from *Accattone*, on the edge of the city, with Franco Citti and Franca Pasut, 1961

4 The River Tagliamento, near Casarsa

5 Filming *Medea* in Cappadocia, 1969

4

5

72

1 The massacre of the innocents
scene from *The Gospel According
to St. Matthew*, 1964

2 Oriental girl, still from *The
Arabian Nights*, 1973

3 Pasolini with Ninetto Davoli
filming *The Decameron*, 1970

4 The three brothers in a still
from *The Decameron*, 1970

5 Pasolini during the filming of
The Arabian Nights, 1973

1

2

3

4

5

1 Pasolini in a working class
  district of Rome, late sixties

2 Filming *The Arabian Nights,* 1973

3 Still from *Accattone,* with Franco
  Citti, 1961

4 Stills from *Comizi d'Amore,* 1963

1

2

3

1

2

3

1 A raven with Marxist views, in a still from *Hawks and Sparrows,* 1965

2 Filming the crucifixion scene in *La ricotta,* 1963, with Laura Betti and Orson Welles

3 Filming the Last Supper scene of *The Gospel According to St. Matthew,* 1964

4 Maria Callas as *Medea,* 1969

5 Procession on the main street of Casarsa

1

2

3

4

1 The election of the most
   beautiful bottom, from *The 120
   Days of Sodom,* 1975

2 Still from *Teorema,* 1968, of
   the erotic encounter between
   Silvana Mangano and Terence
   Stamp as Lucia and the
   mysterious visitor

3 Compar Pietro with his young
   wife Gemmata, still from *The
   Decameron,* 1970

4 Ninetto Davoli as Aziz and the
   "beautiful stranger," stills from
   The Arabian Nights, 1973

Portraits of the soldiers from the massacre of the innoncents, in *The Gospel According to St. Matthew*, 1964

P.P.P.
PIER PAOLO PASOLINI

Prose
Pornography
Parable

Preceding page
Pasolini, c. 1970

The Dreaming Subject

The Motif of the Vision in Pasolini's Work
Roberto Chiesi

"Everything begins now with this dream. A dream, however, that I cannot recall. Everything, rather, *begins again*—if ever anything did begin in my life … in which this something would be something new … "

Pier Paolo Pasolini, *Affabulazione*

The Anomaly as Origin

A visionary narrative is one that "springs from an irrational rationality. It carries the act in which it originates within itself, and that act determines its structure. With its arbitrary character, the anomaly gives rise to the dream and transforms the logic of reality into madness."[1]

These lines are from Pasolini's review of Alberto Moravia's novel *Un'altra vita* (Another Life). At the time they were written, Pasolini was also at work on *Petrolio* (Oil) and directing *Il Fiore delle Mille e una notte* (Flower of the Arabian Nights; the film was known in English simply as *The Arabian Nights*). This "irrational rationality" encapsulates the contradictory elements of the genesis of a visionary story, one that is inspired by an innate anomaly.

The anomaly transgresses and disobeys the laws of the norm; it overruns and undermines them, plunging events into a dreamlike atmosphere and subjecting the logic of the real to madness. It is like the rising of a visceral impulse, the surfacing of a mysterious desire, which inspires the mental projection of a dream and assumes the form of reality, which thus becomes "madness."

An anomaly, explains Pasolini, "is never elementary and consistent; it is never, as it were, of a single piece. At most it is divided into a 'series' of lesser anomalies, whose interconnection brings the anomaly to its salient moment and in doing so determines the course of the narrative. This salient moment of the anomaly—that is, strictly speaking, the anomaly itself—does not always occur at the end of the series, nor does it always appear at the beginning (although these are the two most common cases). Its position in the series is unstable."[2]

These observations may also be applied to the cinematic narrative of the *Fiore delle Mille e una notte*, which recounts a number of interrelated episodes from the Eastern fairy tale of a similar name. In this film, the narrative movements are determined by a series of lesser anomalies,[3] which took place in the past and converge to bring the adventure of Dunia and Taji to its conclusion, an adventure that represents a disguised and specular variant of the movie's principal narrative, the story of Nur ed Din and Zumurrud. In this work, the anomalies of fate—and this is true of both the primary and secondary branches of the narrative—are impossible to decipher; they cannot be "explained." We will never know why Yunan, with the robotic and automatic gestures of a "blind" sleep, kills the adolescent son of a king, nor how it is that Taji knows the missing piece of Dunia's dream.

"There is a moment in which the anomaly and the narrative situation it produces are transformed into a symbol (thus lending an ideological rather than existential meaning to the narrative)."[4] The anomaly's crystallization into a figure, or "symbol," removes it from the "intimate" existential realm of the author and endows it with objective existence as a model, as the emblem of an idea.

"The pure storyteller knows that the Mind that governs human actions and events is powerless to explain its own anomalies. These remain inexplicable, as if to

[1] Pier Paolo Pasolini, "L'inutile sforzo di Moravia per dimostrare l'inesistenza della realtà" (review of Alberto Moravia, *Un'altra vita),* Tempo (October 28, 1973). Also in Pasolini, *Descrizioni di descrizioni* (Turin, 1979), p. 205.

[2] Ibid., p. 206.

[3] The path of the two sons of kings, Shahzaman and Yunan, both marked by remorse for having inadvertently caused the deaths of innocent people, intersects with the destiny of another king's son, Taji Almolup. Taji falls in love with Princess Dunia after meeting Aziz, seeing the painting the young man has kept, and hearing the story of Aziz and Aziza.

[4] Pier Paolo Pasolini, "L'inutile sforzo di Moravia" (see note 1), p. 208.

render all the rest—the material and moral order of life—more explicable."[5] The ontological "difference" of an anomaly remains in the shadow of its unresolved state, and the laws of normality stand out all the more clearly in contrast to it.

It is not only the phenomenon of the anomaly itself that resists attempts to decipher it. The same is true of the mystery contained in the dreams that are inspired by the anomaly. In the tragic poem *Affabulazione* (Mythmaking; written between 1966 and 1970), the father has "a dream, in which / he sees himself loving his son, I do not know in what capacity, / whether as the boy of the father himself, or that of a stranger / who is the father of the father (as a boy) / or the identification with his own mother … No one, / not even I, will ever know this dream. / But it will change the father's entire life."[6] The shadow of Sophocles appears to the father and emphasizes the difference between a "riddle" and a "mystery." Reason is the means for solving riddles, but it is powerless against mysteries like that of the son, who is the reason for the father's disturbing dream: "… reason / is useful indeed in the solving of riddles … / But your son … is not a riddle. / *He is a mystery*."[7] In fact, "… if he were a riddle, / you would surely have solved it. / Either by religion / or by madness, / or finally, as is more likely, / precisely by reason."[8]

The "mystery" cannot be reduced to a riddle, which, afterall can be solved. Words are not sufficient to unlock it and make it manifest. It has fluid and far-reaching outlines, which lie hidden within the secret depths of instincts and impulses, as well as in atavistic and religious rituals. Pasolini confronts the intractable irrationality of the mystery with the mystery of a visionary evocation.

In Pasolini's poetry, the visionary element serves to evoke the mystery that precedes consciousness and birth, imbuing it with a mythical quality. Pasolini's "visions" always have a darkly prophetic character; they always contain the signs of a "curse" that is destined to overtake the subject.

The dreaming subject, who is possessed by the "light" of the vision, is at the mercy of the most irreconcilable and agonizing contradictions. It embraces within its experience "the consummate calm of the contemplative observer and the rapture of one whose intuitions dizzily lead him to the very depths of nature's innocence and abnormality."[9]

The Curse that Precedes Birth

The seventh section of the poem *Una disperata vitalità* (A Desperate Vitality)[10] interrupts the steady flow of the present tense in the verses that precede (and follow) it. The voice of the subject returns to the awful originating moment of "an anomaly of fate," in which the mark of a curse and condemnation lies hidden: "There was a soul, one of those who had yet / to go down into life / … a soul in the light of whose brown eyes / … there burned the desire to die." The "desire to die" refers to an intimate masochistic impulse that pervades Pasolini's work, which is expressed here in the most extreme possible language.

"*He* saw it right away, he / who does not forgive."

[5] Ibid., p. 205.

[6] Pier Paolo Pasolini, "Poeta delle Ceneri" (1966–1967), in *Nuovi Argomenti* (July–December 1980).

[7] Pier Paolo Pasolini, *Affabulazione*, in *Affabulazione, Pilade* (Milan, 1977), p. 68.

[8] Ibid., p. 70.

[9] Pier Paolo Pasolini, "La sventura di non conoscere né Freud né Marx" (review of *Witold Gombrowicz, Journals 1957–1961*), *Tempo* (December 24, 1972), also in Pasolini, *Descrizioni di descrizioni* (see note 1), p. 205.

[10] Published for the first time in *Questo e altro*, March 1964, then in Pasolini, *Poesia in forma di rosa* (Milan, 1964).

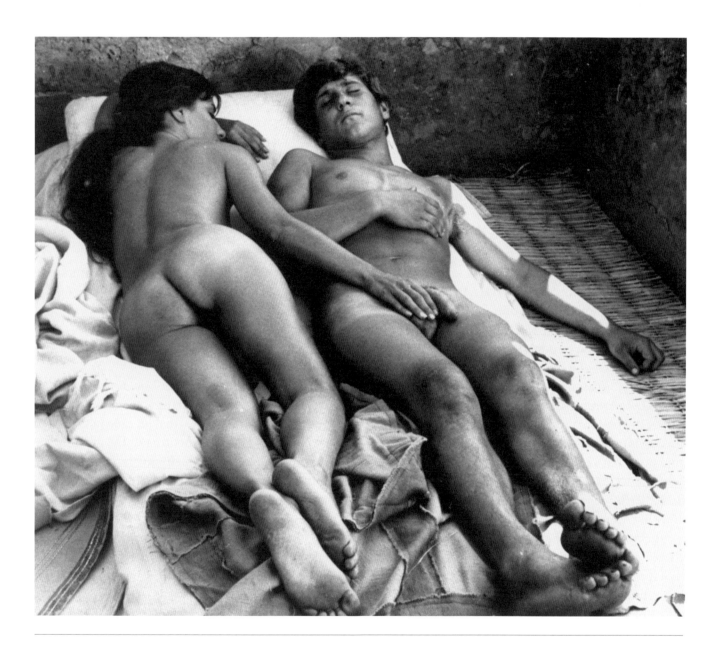

Still from *The Decameron*, 1970

These lines, which are isolated from the surrounding verses, express the ineluctable character of an unfathomable destiny, one that resembles a sentence passed by fate. "He who does not forgive" is identified, not with God, but with a dark and obscure divine being who is a stranger to the Christian notion of forgiveness. Like a religious authority or an incarnation of God, "he placed his hands on its head / and pronounced the curse."

Once again, Pasolini stresses the innocence of the stricken soul: "It was a pure and unblemished soul, like a little boy at first communion." The vision of the myth is overlaid by the concrete image of an everyday religious ritual.

At this point, the intimate secret of the impulse mentioned above, the masochistic trait that lies deep in the subject's identity, reappears "with, in its feeble eyes, the desire to die." Pasolini also returns to the terrible moment in which the soul was "seen," or rather chosen, by the one "who does not forgive," prefiguring the poet's lifelong temperamental character; it is an attitude with a touch of the oxymoron about it: "he saw an infinite capacity to obey / and an infinite capacity to rebel."

The verses in which Pasolini describes the innocent gaze of the soul—"which looked at him trustingly / as a lamb looks at its just executioner"—seem to recall the scene from the film *Medea* (1969) in which the pure, defenseless smile of the youth who is sacrificed at the annual agricultural festival of fertility in Colchis. The subject's "executioner" is "just" because he contains an echo of the Easter priest, whose role it is to sacrifice the lamb.

Suddenly the poet illuminates the gaze of the anonymous divinity: "the light disappeared / from its eyes, and there rose a shadow of pity." This shadow introduces the most horrible lines, which contain the curse that will overwhelm the subject's destiny: "You will go down into the world, / and you will be immaculate and kind, even-tempered and true; / you will have an infinite capacity to obey / and an infinite capacity to rebel. / You will be pure. / Therefore I curse you." The last two verses contain the dark threat of the prophecy, which finds expression in a cruelly contradictory judgment. The subject's purity is rewarded, not with a blessing, but with a curse.

As if recounting an actual experience, Pasolini describes the special light in the eyes of the divine being, who looks at the soul as he curses it: "I still see his gaze / full of pity—and that slight hint of horror / that we feel for the one who arouses it." The pity in the eyes of the dark, anonymous being is overlaid with the horror of its victim, who arouses his pity because it is condemned and marked by a terrible fate. "The gaze with which one follows / one who is going to his death but does not know it, / and to whom, by a necessity that constrains both the one who knows and the one who doesn't know, / one says nothing." The "necessity" is that of a superior will, a superior order whose judgments are final, and which makes for the ineluctable character of this "vision." "I still see his gaze, / as I moved away / —from Eternity— toward my birthplace." The subject is disturbed to discover the light of a horrible compassion in the eyes of the being who has condemned him. This light is unbearable because it allows the subject to divine the horror of the destiny that awaits.

The Expulsion from the Two Gardens of Paradise

In 1966 Pasolini published the *Teoria dei due paradisi*,[11] a poem that he originally intended to include in *La Divina Mimesis*.[12] Two years later, he incorporated a revised version of the same poem into the novel *Teorema* (Theorem, 1968). In this novel, an upper middle class family is visited by a stranger who seduces everyone in the family, plus the maid, and then disappears. The poem functions, in the context of the novel, as a poetic interlude to Odetta, the daughter, who is deeply devoted to the cult of her father, who, like all the members of her family, is deeply upset by the visitor. Pasolini originally intended the two paradises to be those of neo-capitalism and communism, but the meaning of the poem changed completely as he wrote it. In its finished form, it represents the mythical dimension of the first years of life, expressed in the language of dreams. "The first paradise was that of the father. / All the senses were united / in the exclusive adoration of something erect, in this world / that had but one single feature, like the desert, / a golden, leonine color, warmed by an unknown sex, / like a star of which the light alone remains / —it was the season of the sun."

It is the mythical moment of physical fusion with the father, in which the father's (hetero)sexuality was the quality in which the child found protection. The image of the desert—so prominent in Pasolini's films of this time, from *Il Vangelo secondo Matteo* (The Gospel

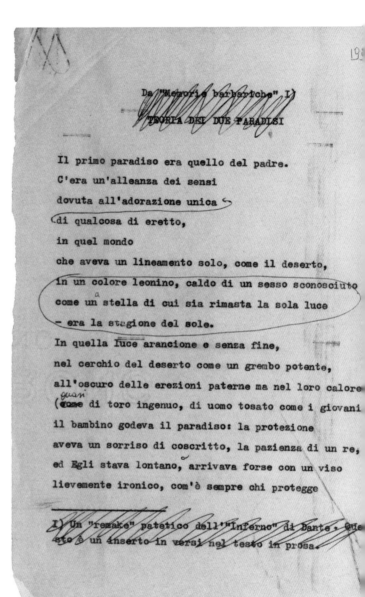

[11] *Comma. Prospettive di cultura* 5 (October–November 1966), pp. 34–37.

[12] A trace of the poem still remains in Canto II: "[A] barbaric work, in which the Two Paradises are nothing but a foolish and childish theory?" Comp. *La Divina Mimesis* (Turin, 1975), p. 24.

Teoria dei due paradisi, 1966
Typescript
Gabinetto Scientifico Letterario
G. P. Vieusseux, Florence

200

il debole, il tenerino – ch'è quasi una donna.

L'odio sorse improvviso, e senza ragione.

Il bambino odiò forse quell'uomo

per la sua troppa innocenza.

Il grembo ch'era come un sole coperto da nuvole

dolci e potenti, il grembo di quell'uomo lontano,

divenne un oscuro fondo di calzoni,

forse s'immiserì, perdette l'innocenza equina,

non fu che umano. E il bambino obbedì.

Venne il giorno che cade fuori dalle lontananze

arancione del deserto,

si vedono i primi palmizi,

la prima pista che si perde muta fra le dune.

E il bambino perdette il paradiso.

Il padre lo cacciò, punendolo

per il suo desiderio di essere punito:

obbedì anch'egli dell'obbedienza del figlio

(anch'egli aveva un padre?).

Quel primo paradiso restò così nel deserto

di una verde regione,

o di una piccola città di provincia

– nelle case dalle tende bianche di una nonna paterna,

ad altezze impossibili, dove per sempre fu perso

201

il calore della fecondità del padre ragazzo.

Il bambino cadde a capofitto sulla terra,

perdette il nome di Lucifero e prese, insieme,

quello di Abele e quello di Caino (così fu almeno

nelle terre

tra l'ultimo biancheggiare del mare

e il primo rosa dei deserti africani).

Era il nuovo paradiso, e in mezzo

a primule e viole

c'era la madre con la sua pelliccia povera

odorata di precoce primavera.

Com'era terrestre, dolcemente terrestre

la sua dolcezza di bambina, che non ha

orizzonte diverso da quello

che i genitori, o i fratelli, o il marito le assegnano:

e rassegnata, e piena di fantasia,

sogna, oltre quell'orizzonte, terre solo più felici,

ed eroiche,

senza osare desiderarle per sè,

ma desiderandole solo per quel figlietto al suo fianco,

anche lui tutto imperlato del fresco delle primule.

Scorreva un fiume, in quel paradiso,

e ognuno può dargli il nome che vuole,

ognuno ha il suo, ch'è sempre lo stesso,

According to St. Matthew) to *Teorema* and *Porcile* (Pigsty)—represents a vision of the world still rooted in a uniform physiognomy, which has its god in the figure of the father.

Just as in *Una disperata vitalità,* an innocent character, a little boy, is dependent on the smile of a superior being—in this case the father—who, in the *Teoria dei due paradisi,* is described as wearing "a slightly ironic expression, as is always the case with one who protects / a weak and delicate creature, who is almost a woman," but this initial moment of harmony between the son and the father is suddenly shattered: "hate arose, suddenly and without reason. / Perhaps the child hated the man / because he was too innocent."

In the film *Edipo re* (Oedipus Rex; 1967), which Pasolini made not quite a year after writing this poem, it is the father who hates the son, because the son has come to steal the mother's love from him. In the poem *Teoria dei due paradisi,* the opposite is the case. It is the son who hates the father because of his ignorance, his pathetic naïveté ("innocence"). The sex of "that distant man," so powerful in its prominence and sensuality, "became a dark seat of the pants / and perhaps it wilted and weakened, lost its equine innocence, / and was merely human." The father lost his godlike aura, his zoomorphic and superhuman aspect, appearing instead in all the mediocrity of his merely human features. "And the child obeyed." These lines, with their definitive tone, echo the "infinite capacity to obey" of the subject in *Una disperata vitalità.* Here too, this obedience introduces a curse, for "the child lost paradise. / The father drove him

out, punishing him / for his desire to be punished: / he too obeyed with the obedience of the son."

"The desire to be punished" is once again the masochistic impulse, which makes the son "different" from the father and constitutes a hallmark of his homosexuality. Yet the father too—like the figure "who does not forgive" in *Una disperata vitalità*—obeys a "necessity."

The first paradise now takes on the appearance of a mythical Friuli, where "the warmth of the boy father's fertility" was "lost forever"—where the father faded from view—but which was also the place where the son discovered the incontrovertible fact of his own homosexuality. Like Lucifer, the child fell to earth, but he "lost the name of Lucifer and took both / that of Abel and that of Cain," a dual name together with a dual identity, like "Pier" and "Paolo" or the "doubles" of the author's unfinished novel *(Petrolio)* or youthful play *(I Turcs tàl Friùl* [The Turks in Friuli]).

The new paradise is the earth, which stands wholly under the aegis of the love and physicality of the mother: "there, among primroses and violets, / was the mother with her ragged animal skin, / smelling of early spring. / How sweet and earthly / was her sweetness; it was that of a little girl, who knows no / other horizon than that / which is assigned to her by her parents or her brothers or her husband."

It is the paradise of a mother devoted exclusively to her son, who is also "all beaded with the freshness of the primroses." The "new paradise" of the mother is the fabulous, mythical image of a landscape in which various

Pasolini with his mother
Susanna Colussi, 1924

Pasolini with his father
Carlo Alberto, 1938

natural scenes return again and again: the countryside, the sea, and a carpet of fruit and flowers.

Over all of it reigns the sun, while the new father is consigned to the silence and anonymity of the background. Suddenly this edenic, idyllic scene is invaded by something dark and unnamed—the "shocking scandal"—which the mother must painfully accept. The "scandal" lay concealed in the desperate song of a nightingale (a reference to the collection of poems in Friulian dialect *L'usignolo della chiesa cattolica* [The Nightingale of the Catholic Church], written between 1943 and 1949) "at the edge of paradise."

Once again, "the same hate without reason" bursts forth onto the scene. In this case, it recalls the "transgression" of original sin in the earthly paradise. Later, a number of verses discuss the source of this hate and the reasons for the scandal. It is the mad identification with "those whom something that is enormously ours places next to us," that is, the mother. "Thus, we were the mother who sins before the fruit of sorrow without forgiveness, unknown to us, who were terrified by its mystery."

The fruit is an obvious reference to the forbidden fruit of the Book of Genesis, and it alludes to the mystery of "impure" sexuality, the mystery of homosexuality. The landscape of countryside and sea now disappears, and the desert returns, with its "deep silence."

In the moment of original sin, the subject identifies absolutely with the mother's sexuality: "the mother, *who was her child*, / bit into that summer fruit / with the innocence of a mother and the malice of a son."

A similar identification is described in *Affabulazione*, in the verses that refer to the father's dream. The figure of the father returns. While it is no longer assimilated to the flaming sun of the first paradise, here too it is the target of the subject's identification: *"With him too we had identified."* Perhaps the poet is alluding to the father's blazing sensuality, his powerful eroticism. "We sinned with their mouths, with their hands." The fall from the second paradise is caused by the "different" nature of the eroticism and of the acts in which that eroticism is expressed. In its own actions and impulses, the subject recognizes a matrix in which the sexual identities of the mother and the father merge.

To mark the end of the second paradise, Pasolini inserts a precise autobiographical reference: "Holding our mother's hand, / we set out upon the paths of the world." It is the journey from Casarsa to Rome that the author made with his mother on January 28, 1950, which marked his definitive departure from Friuli and his move to the capital city. "Lucifer parted from Abel / and followed his destiny / into deepest darkness. / Abel died, / killed by himself under the name of Cain. / Thus only one son remained, / *a single son.*"

The subject's division into multiple souls and its definitive separation from a self that is suppressed by this journey again assume biblical trappings. In fact, the suppression of this "personality" did bring about the fusion into a single individual and his "initiation" to Rome, "where the first seeding took place twelve thousand years ago." The son has left his childhood and youth behind him. He is a man who—fallen from paradise—must deal with the trials and tribulations of supporting himself. "We had to earn our living: / this took us from ourselves, and was and is the first hell—this, yes, this is what you remember."

This "hell" is probably an image of the present, "in which you live, although you do not know it." The difficult and precarious conditions of the subject's existence in Rome produce a transformation, in which a "poor son / with a false image of himself" is forced to wear himself out working for a living, in a daily life "where work / … is a necessity of life that annihilates life." These autobiographical elements become the symbol of a human condition that weighs particularly heavily on the working classes (this is perhaps the single element of the author's original intentions that survives in the finished text).

In 1968, the poet revises these verses and incorporates them into the novel *Teorema*. In the poem *Il primo paradiso, Odetta …* (The First Paradise, Odetta …), he attributes the adoration of the father, which dominates the first years of the subject's life, to Odetta. In fact, however, this identification only lasts the first few lines of the poem, because the focus immediately shifts to the brother, Pietro, "who is of the same sex as God." It is he who discovers his hatred for the father.

Some of the changes that Pasolini made to the original poem of 1966 accentuate the dreamlike character discussed above: "Thus, the child crossed the border of the First Paradise, / which remained behind in time; as the *dreamed* time of a verdant region lined with transparent rows of poplar trees." The time of the first paradise is assimilated to a dreamlike dimension, which is condensed into the image of a changeless and pristine desert landscape.[13]

Affabulazione: The Riddle and Mystery of a Dream

In the tragedy *Affabulazione*, the "dreamer" who suffers the onslaught of the visions is a middle-aged man (Pasolini is forty-four when he begins work on the play) and a father. He has a feverish dreamlike vision, which disturbs him deeply and determines the entire course of the drama. His vision is never described in its entirety, but it appears in evocative fragments in the few words spoken by the father in his sleep. These words reveal his fear of physical contact and the violence of a sudden desire: "I want to touch your knees … / Behind your knee … your tendons!"

As Walter Siti and Silvia De Laude have pointed out, these lines "explicitly" echo "the passage from the *Quaderni rossi* [Red Notebooks] that Pasolini himself has described as the founding myth of his own homosexuality."[14] Still more explicit in this regard are the lines from the vision in *Affabulazione* in which the father evokes a "boy who plays, a big boy!"

In one of the subsequent verses—"Where are you going … boy, my father!"—the body of a desired boy is identified with the figure of the father. This line sheds light on the difficult passage from the *Teoria dei due paradisi* in which the poet evokes the union of all the senses ("All the senses were united") and the myth of the father's body. The line: "Aaaaaah, / here I have the feet, the little feet of a three-year-old child," alludes to

13 The description of the son's "fall" and the evocation of the second paradise take up verses of the earlier poem with alterations that are essentially merely formal. In the final verses, Pasolini explains why "I have spoken of your brother Pietro and not of you," and anticipates the madness that awaits Odetta after the Guest's departure.

14 Walter Siti and Silvia De Laude, "Note e notizie sui testi," in Pier Paolo Pasolini, *Pier Paolo Pasolini: Tutte le Opere: Per il teatro*, ed. Walter Siti and Silvia De Laude (Milan, 2001), p. 1178.

Oedipus's "swollen little feet" (this touch of Sophocles summarizes the plot of the Greek dramatist's tragedy almost in its entirety). Then the father's voice expresses a regression to childhood. He calls for his mother and says that he wants to run after the boy and cannot be without him. It is the reconstruction of a primitive and infantile romantic crisis, which is homosexual in nature.

The father's vision is a dream that has enlightened him, but he is unable to grasp the "truth" it has revealed about him. After first being deeply upset by the dream—"a spirit came down into a body in the grip of demonic possession"—he now continues to torment himself, realizing that "it is in my son / that my dream continues!" His dream is "a religious dream, / in which I heard a call / that now defies my efforts to remember it."

Later on, the connection to the visions of *Una disperata vitalità* and *Teoria dei due paradisi* becomes even clearer. Like the subject of the poems of 1963 and 1966, the father has dreamed of a divine being. "I know very well what I dreamed / that damned afternoon! I dreamed You. / That is why my life has changed." The father's "madness" is the desire to know and possess the mystery of the son—his youth, his sex—"and I must not seek to *solve* it, for it is not a riddle, / but to *know* it— that is, touch it, see it, hear it— / for it is a mystery …"[15] In order to do so he must go by way of the body and physical contact, in an identification between his own father and the son and in a reversal of his own identity: "… that dream / of which I remember only that

there were / a station, my father, a boy, / public gardens, blond."[16] The father kills the son, as if he were carrying out a mythical filicide. But "rather than / want to kill my son… / I wanted to be killed by him!! / … And he, rather than want to kill me / or be killed by me, / willing and resigned, / … did not want to kill me or be killed by me!!"

Like Julian, his contemporary in *Porcile,* the son in *Affabulazione* is in fact neither obedient nor disobedient. His death at his father's hands will bring about the father's decline, leaving him a derelict and a beggar. Above all, however, it turns him into one who is compelled to recount again and again the story of a tragedy that never ends.

Film as a Prophecy of Death

Some of the characters in Pasolini's films are also dominated by these visions, with their "dark" revelations. However, the dream sequences Pasolini imagined and elaborated in his screenplays are not always present in the films. This is because, as we shall see, a number of sequences were never actually shot, and of those that were, some were not included in the final cuts. In Pasolini's films, the dreamers often witness the revelation of their own death, which appears to them clothed in the "displacements," masquerades, and riddles of their visions.

The dream that unfolds in *Accattone* (1961) contains dark forebodings of the fate that awaits the film's protagonist, but it also conveys a few secret and intimate traits of his personality buried deep in his unconscious

---

15 Pier Paolo Pasolini, *Affabulazione* (see note 7), p. 75.

16 Ibid., p. 91.

mind. It is no accident that Vittorio Cataldi, known as Accattone (or Beggar), has his dream at a moment when his face is "disfigured by blows,"[17] in a sleep without rest, soon after being beaten up by the other pimps, with whom he had associated at the beginning of the film.

Accattone has never belonged to the world of normality (his attempts to find employment in a job of some kind very quickly came to nought), and now he no longer even belongs to the underworld of the pimps. He is alone.

In his nightmare, he has a role within the vision, but at the same time that he is a character, he is also a spectator. He witnesses the apparition of the Neopolitan brothers, who sit on the ground and greet him completely naturally, as if in reality. In the following shot, however, he sees their corpses, naked, bloody, and covered in rubble like dead bodies after a massacre or disaster. The image of these dead bodies heralds the vision that will appear to him shortly thereafter. It is the discovery of his own death, which occurs off-screen and is not made tangible by an image of his corpse. It is a death accepted as real, reported in the few words exchanged by the other pimps, who speak to him as if he were both himself and someone else. Accattone's former companions are wearing dark suits, appropriate dress for a funeral, and Accattone suddenly realizes that he too is wearing identical funeral attire.

Just as he cannot see his own dead body, he is also forbidden to enter the cemetery. Instead he must behave like a boy, disobeying the order and climbing over the

wall to enter the place where his corpse is to be buried. He arrives in time to find the gravedigger at his task. He asks him to bury him in the sun and not in the shade, not in the dark earth. He does not, he says, wish to be banished, in death as in life, to a place of exile where there is no hope of salvation. (This is a religious allusion that refers to the citation from Dante at the beginning of the film). Accattone's nightmare prefigures his death, which is banal and accidental. He falls off his motorcycle while attempting to escape after a robbery. He dies like a dog and at last finds relief in ceasing to exist.

The same elements of premonition and revelation return in a number of sequences imagined by Pasolini in the screenplay for *Mamma Roma* (1962), sequences he did not go on to shoot.

In these unfilmed sequences, Ettore, the central character's adolescent son, experiences a protracted vision that turns out in the end to be an expression of the resentment he feels toward his mother and a prophecy

[17] Pier Paolo Pasolini, *Accattone* (Rome, 1961), p. 105.

The levitation miracle, still from *Teorema*, 1968

of death. He first has this vision after reacting violently to the approach of a homosexual, in a section that was shot but not included by Pasolini in the final version of the film:

"In an unfamiliar place, at a deserted stop, Ettore gets out and walks down an unfamiliar street, lined with sad little gardens blazing in the sun. As he walks on, he turns a corner and there, advancing upon him from a huge arterial road, he sees a row of elephants. They move forward, slow, huge, moving their limbs as if swimming, as if in slow motion, navigating as if suspended in the sunlit space of the avenue, waving their enormous ears and lifting their trunks."[18]

The second time he sees them, he is already in the throes of fever, and he is about to enter the hospital to commit a robbery, the hospital where he will be captured and where he will die: "a number of elephants, which walk toward him slowly and terribly, taking a path that is unrecognizable—street or tundra—lifting their trunks … while his friends go on talking off-screen."[19]

Lying on a bed in the hospital where he had gone to commit a robbery, "with burning eyes, he sees."[20] Ettore's vision was to have been interspersed with images of a patient humming "Violino tzigano" (Gypsy violin; the same song to which the boy had danced with his mother) and overlaid with another patient's recital of Canto XVIII of Dante's *Commedia*.

Ettore "sees" four or five elephants advancing upon Guidonia, where he had lived as a child before his mother came to get him and take him to Rome with

her. The pachyderms raise their trunks in Ettore's direction, but they make for the mother. This scene is once again accompanied by the voices of the patients as they paraphrase Dante's verses. The vision is triggered by Ettore's "evil, and at the same time, frightened looks." The elephants charge Mamma Roma, who is on a little bridge, terrified, while the son tries to warn her of the danger. Ettore does not witness the conclusion of the tragedy, because it is hidden from view by the masses of the elephants' bodies and the dust. After the elephants have passed, however, we see the "dead body of Mamma Roma, lying in the dust like a paltry blackish rag."

Pasolini intended to overlay this scene of the film with the voices of the patients as they snicker at a joke that one of them has told, like a ghastly and strident

---

[18] Pier Paolo Pasolini, *Mamma Roma* (Milan, 1962), p. 66.

[19] Ibid., p. 108.

[20] Ibid., p. 117.

The vision of the slain brothers, still from *Accatone*, 1961 counter-melody. Ettore's frenzied and feverish reaction—he leaps out of bed and runs screaming toward the door—is triggered precisely by the horror of this vision and his own sense of remorse at the dim awareness of having desired it. To prevent him from acting similarly in the future, Ettore is strapped to the bed in the isolation ward, where he dies. Thus, the vision is not only prophetic; it is also the indirect cause of Ettore's death.

In *Il Decameron* (The Decameron, 1971), the content of the nocturnal vision of Giotto's student, who suddenly awakens and raises his head to look around, "is the hereafter. It is a frontal vision, naïve and yet terrible and fascinating. In the middle is the Madonna holding the Christ child in her arms, while choirs of angels and saints behold her on either side." Beneath them, however, yawns a vision of hell, with hairy devils mistreating the souls who dwell there. Giotto's student (who is played by Pasolini himself) has this vision in a half-sleep, one that coincides with that of Tingoccio, a character in another story, who, as we learn at the end of the vision, has already died as a result of his erotic excesses.

It is interesting to note that at first this otherworldly vision seems to be dominated by God the father; as the camera moves in, however, we see the face of the Madonna (Silvana Mangano). The supreme bliss mingles with the horror of hell's torments, while the radiant smile of the Madonna shines above. It is impossible not to glimpse a secret, prophetic aura in this "revelation" of the hereafter in the middle of the night.

Another otherworldly vision occurs in *I racconti di Canterbury* (The Canterbury Tales; 1972), shortly before the epilogue of the film. In this case, the "dreamer" is a greedy, hypocritical friar, who is "visited" by an angel as he lies sleeping, surrounded by food of every kind. The winged figure escorts him to hell. By contrast with the vision of the painter in *Il Decameron,* who lay in bed and watched the magnificent otherworldly epiphany unfold before him, in this case the observer—the corrupt and pleasure-seeking friar—is physically involved in the grotesque and terrifying spectacle of the denizens of hell. The friar is assailed on his visit to hell by the din of Malebolge (Dante's eighth circle of hell). The demons deride him with lewd gestures, and he watches in terror as Satan defecates, disgorging the friars from his gigantic anus and passing gas with a thunderous noise. The friar's vision clearly foreshadows the fate that is in store for him; it is the image of his imminent damnation.

In *Il Fiore delle Mille e una notte* (1974), Princess Dunia's dream forms part of the story told by Munis, a girl, to her sisters and Nur e Din, their guest and secret partner for their sexual pleasure. The dream is a painful and bitter one. A female dove has rescued a male from a trap, but when she is trapped in a bird net in her turn, the male does not help her. As a result of this dream, Dunia decides to have no further dealings with men. She embroiders a rich and precious tapestry depicting two gazelles. It is this same tapestry that Aziza leaves to Aziz upon her death; it comes into his possession on the same day that he truly understands the meaning of the love his cousin had borne him. It is thus a magical

Princess Dunia's dream, still
from *The Arabian Nights,* 1973

Yunan's vision, still from
The Arabian Nights, 1973

object, a kind of talisman linking two distant stories. It leads Taji Almolup to fall in love with Dunia without ever having seen her, and it prompts him to create the mosaic containing all the elements of her dream. The mosaic reveals that the male dove, who the princess believed had acted out of cowardice, had actually been seized and killed by a bird of prey. "Dreams are sometimes poor teachers, Dunia, because the whole truth is never contained in a single dream. The whole truth is contained in many dreams." This is one of the rare dreams in Pasolini's work that is unclouded by any obscurity; it is crystal clear and "enlightening."

Another dream, which we are not intended to see, is that of Yunan, the young prince who, like an agent of destiny, discovers the underground refuge of the fifteen-year-old son of a king. In his sleep—like a sleepwalker or an automaton—Yunan kills the boy by stabbing him in the back. He keeps his eyes closed as he does so, as if possessed by a vision that he alone can see. It is a vision that takes objective form in his real and concrete act, an act of death. The story seems to point to the existence of a deadly curse, which not only leads to the death of the king's son, but also destroys the cheerful and serene homosexual erotic bond that has spontaneously sprung up between the two boys.

Medea and the Visions of Primitive Ritual

For *Medea* (1969), Pasolini imagined and filmed a number of visionary sequences that he decided to leave out of the final version. Fortunately, these have been at least partially preserved.[21] The film itself contains

only a single vision, which foreshadows the deadly spell that Medea will cast upon Glauce, Jason's prospective bride.

The first vision was to have followed the moment in which Jason has abandoned Medea and she falls into a profound crisis. It is the second crisis to overtake her after the flight from Colchis and the sacred world to which she belongs so completely, and it is the definitive one. At first her love of Jason had compensated her for her religious loss, but now she "again loses any possible connection with reality, which becomes a nightmarish place for her, a prison, a merely physical space without any meaning."[22] She notices that "the whole house is full of animals: sheep, goats, cows, dogs, and birds, as well as a bull that is lowing terribly and mating with a

---

[21] Collectively titled *Visioni della Medea* (Visions of Medea), the sequences are combined with a number of alternate takes and last about forty minutes. They are currently in the possession of Cinemazero di Pordenone and have been released on DVD by Carlotta Films.

[22] Pier Paolo Pasolini, *Medea* (Milan, 1970), p. 63

Silvana Mangano as the Madonna, still from *The Decameron*, 1970 cow (but all that can be seen of him is his raised head, which seems to be made of fire)."

The next dream is a nightmare. Medea is digging in Colchis while two men, "with the unfathomable irony of dreams, horribly winking,"[23] prepare to carry out a human sacrifice. The victim, who is stretched out naked on the ground, has no face. Medea digs, but she is unable to break the earth, while the two men, without speaking, exhort her to hurry. The men kill the victim and then quarter and butcher the body, while they indicate to Medea—laughing and expressing themselves with "guttural sounds," in a "language of dreams"—that she is to wait. The sorceress watches as they remove the victim's heart and feed on it, drinking the blood. The scene is a variation on the fertility rite in which the sorceress had actively participated in Colchis. In the nightmare, however, Medea is reduced to passivity; she is merely a mute presence watching the scene of a human sacrifice. She herself will later carry out the most gruesome of human sacrifices, murdering her own children to avenge herself against Jason.

Then Medea is in her house in Corinth, and the sun appears to her in human form. A doubling occurs. One Medea, "regal," expresses herself in the verses of Euripides and "speaks in that manner, formidable and daunting, to the serving women, modern, thirsting for vengeance, confident, mistress of herself and of reality; while another Medea observes, a Medea who is trembling, anxious, miserable, and beseeching, and who is not ashamed to exhibit her terrible fear and insecurity as she watches events unfold."[24]

Medea then becomes one again and beholds a series of wonders, which Pasolini describes as "the resurrection of bodies." A seed that sprouts and becomes a plant. Medea, who changes into "a single enormous eye."[25] However, this is not a seed that grows and changes underground, but bloody human limbs, which come together to form a complete human body. Mice come out of the openings and are transformed into human beings with masks, the dead. *"Medea's lone eye watches like an enormous fish."* The chariot of the sun comes down to get her, and Medea climbs into it with her two children.

In this vision too, Medea is a passive presence, reduced to the sole activity of watching. She is present at the rituals of mysteries that refer to eschatology, the other world, and death. Pasolini writes in the screenplay for *Medea* that "the sun is both the god of fertility and the god of death."[26]

The sun returns in Medea's second dream, and once again the sorceress is split in two, "one in bed beside her sleeping lover, anxious and imploring, and another who follows" the sun. This vision takes place after Medea has made love to Jason (after their actual relationship has ended), and it precedes the prophetic vision of the deadly gift to Glauce, a dress entrusted to the sorceress by the sun. The presence of the god in the film—which was to have included the sound of his voice—would have made the divine inspiration of Medea's spell more explicit.

The vision of the deadly gift to Glauce, which Pasolini retains in the final version of the film, is a prophecy

---

23 Ibid., p. 64.

24 Ibid., p. 67.

25 Ibid., p. 69.

26 Ibid., p. 72.

of the crime and the vengeance that the sorceress wishes
to take against the woman with whom Jason has fallen
in love, against her father, and also, indirectly, against
the Argonaut himself. Its recurrence in the film, with a
number of (not insignificant) differences, heightens the
cruelty of Medea's act, which becomes like a ritual first
carried out in imagination, as Medea hatches her plan,
and then, brutally, in reality. Medea's visions are giddy
emanations of the savage, archaic, and esoteric universe
from which the sorceress comes. They seize her and
guide her actions, like the inspirations of an arcane and
bloodthirsty deity.

The Apocalypse of the Present

In Pasolini's last film, *Salò o le 120 giornate di Sodoma*
(Salò, or the 120 Days of Sodom; 1975), a number of
young men and women are carried off by military un-
derlings to an isolated estate, where four monstrous so-
called gentlemen—a duke ("Duca"), a bishop, a magis-
trate, and a president—have come together to torture,
humiliate, and kill their victims. In this work the visions
take the form of "spectacles" involving the executioners, their accomplices, and their victims. These are the
entr'actes in which the narrators—four prostitutes—tell
stories of perversion, and the four monsters are immediately inspired to act them out, using their henchmen
as the instruments and their victims as the objects.
The film's long series of horrors culminates in the final
massacre, which the "gentlemen" observe from high up
in a palazzo, sitting on a high-backed chair behind a
window. They watch through a pair of binoculars that

Maria Callas and Pasolini
on the set of *Medea,* 1969

look like opera glasses, which the duke suddenly turns around in order to look through the wrong end. The atrocities that the four monsters take turns observing constitute the final episode of the game they have supervised and directed throughout the film, torturing and selecting their victims until they have eliminated those who have turned out to be unreceptive to their pedagogy.

Thus, the "drowned" are the young men and women who end up naked, debased, and slaughtered by the deadly acts of torture in the courtyard. The "saved" are those young people who take their place beside the monsters to observe the spectacle of the "final solution." These terrible images of rape, hanging, amputation, burning, and scalping carry the visions of hell already staged by Pasolini in *Il Decameron* and *I Racconti di Canterbury* to their furthest and most outrageous possible point.

The difference is that in *Salò,* it is not the damned souls of sinners that are tortured, but the bodies of the young men and women who have not succeeded in adapting and joining the ranks of the new order, the new way of being human that is imposed by the four "monsters." The hell that is staged in the courtyard of *Salò* becomes a hallucinatory space, in which the accomplices play with the implements of torture, while the four gentlemen carry out loathsome acts, yelling, screaming, and laughing derisively, in addition to parading themselves in a grotesque and ridiculous variety-show ballet.

It is a masquerade, a ritual that alludes to something else, like a medieval mystery play. This vision, which takes place not in a dream, but in a performance space, where the spectacle is horribly identical with the reality of the actions carried out in it, refers to the medieval iconography of the torments of hell. Above all, however, it refers to the destruction of Italy's culture, one of the principal and most painfully obsessive themes of Pasolini's *Scritti corsari* (Corsair Pages) and *Lettere luterane* (Lutheran Letters).

At issue is the process, denounced by Pasolini, in which the Italians were forced into mass conformity with petite-bourgeois models in the 1970s, as well as their brutalization by television and consumerism, which slowly but surely came to dominate all areas of Italian society.

In *Edipo re* (1967), the part of the film devoted to the myth had the quality of a great, sweeping vision, which blurred the sharp outlines of an autobiographical recollection that occupied the first moments of the film. By contrast, in his last, unrealized cinematic project— *Porno-teo-kolossal*[27]—Pasolini's vision was to have been coextensive with the film itself. The film describes the long journey of Nunzio, an old Magus who—accompanied by his servant, Epifanio—has long awaited the "call" of the comet, which at long last appears to him to signal the birth of the Messiah. He pursues it through three symbolic cities—Sodom (1950s Rome, where homosexuality reigns); Gomorrah (Milan in 1975, which is dominated by heterosexuality); and Numanzia (a socialist Paris of the near future, under siege by a fascist technocratic army)—until he reaches Ur, his

[27] Pier Paolo Pasolini, "Porno-teo-kolossal," *Cinecritica* 13 (April–June 1989), pp. 33–53, also in Walter Siti and Franco Zabagli, ed., *Pier Paolo Pasolini. Tutte le Opere: Per il cinema,* (Milan, 2001). Pasolini planned to shoot the film in spring 1976.

Still from *The 120 Days of Sodom,*
1975

final destination, where he discovers that utopia does not actually exist.

Epifanio and Nunzio bear witness to horrific situations, terrible collective rituals, especially in Gomorrah, a city that is emblematic of the devastating forced "standardization" that Pasolini saw taking place in Italy. It is no accident that it is also a metropolis dominated by the Moloch of television, which would have appeared for the first time in Pasolini's films. In the two biblical cities, an anomaly—a transgression of the respective cities' sexual norms—triggers an immediate repressive reaction by the authorities (milder in Sodom, ruthless and inhuman in Gomorrah), and an execution in the context of a collective ritual. Not long after, a catastrophe erupts, which overtakes and annihilates the city.

Epifanio never sees the mysterious and ineluctable unfolding of the anomalous event that gives rise to the chain of dramatic consequences, which in turn attract the nemesis of destruction. He is sleeping when it takes place. However, he was to have experienced the vision of the barbarity and imminent apocalypse that are in store.

At the same time that he was preparing and filming *Salò,* with its circles of hell, Pasolini was also transfiguring Italy's decline in the visions of the figure of Merda in the unfinished pages of *Petrolio.* They are visions of "pure and simple physical presence,"[28] the body of the Italians of "six or seven years ago," which Pasolini juxtaposes with the current state of degeneration (in 1975).

It is a present whose hallmarks are ugliness and disgust, whose model is hidden from view, because the sight of it would be "unbearable." It is a present marked by the triumph of conformity, by "the absence of a Model and hence disorientation and sickness," by disavowal, bourgeois respectability, bourgeois dignity, "the Word of American-style hedonism and materialism."[29]

The new humanity has new ideals, and "its ideal of life is represented by the professionals and employees, who plunder and steal. The void left behind by the life that has ebbed from their bodies—like water that dries up and, as it does so, leaves the shore full of stinking garbage—is filled by bourgeois, professional, technical, organizational dignity, whose vulgarity, together with the wretchedness that lingers in these bodies, gives off the holy horror of a tortured and murdered body."[30]

---

[28] Pier Paolo Pasolini, *Petrolio* (Turin, 1992), p. 330.

[29] Ibid., p. 354.

[30] Ibid., pp. 370–371.

Roberto Chiesi *is a film critic and curator of the Centro Studi – Archivio Pier Paolo Pasolini in Bologna, and has published articles on Federico Fellini and Pier Paolo Pasolini.*

P.P.P.

PIER PAOLO PASOLINI

Pamphlet
Poem
Parody

Preceding page
Pasolini at a football match, 1960s

Transmediality and Pastiche

Techniques in Pasolini's Art Production
Benjamin Meyer-Krahmer

"I was a 'seven-year-old poet' like Rimbaud," boasted Pasolini at the top of his written work, *Who is Me*, in 1966, thereby ranking himself among the great poets.[1] Literature and life merged.

In the autobiographical perspective of the text, his first period in Rome became a retrospective experience of a page of a book, and his way of life, a poem. "I lived this page of a novel, the only novel in my life: / for the rest, what the hell, / I lived lyrically like any obsessive."[2]

In his self-descriptions as *Il Poeta delle ceneri* (The Poet of Ashes), as he later called *Who is Me,* Pasolini interwove text and life, excitingly combining the stylized and the profane in a magic combination of autobiography and poetry. Writing is invoked as *the* link with the world—it is both an escape route and a description: "In poetry, there was an answer to everything."[3] But at the time he wrote *Who is Me,* his firm belief in writing already belonged to the past. By the mid-sixties at the latest, Pasolini was convinced that the writers of his day—including himself—did not have the language to address the current political, social, or historical situation. In his essay "The End of the Avant-Garde," published in 1966, he observed in a kind of global, sociopolitical stocktaking of a conclusion: "There is probably no one who does not notice that this enumeration of worldwide phenomena is no longer in any way connected with the literary avant-garde. That's just it."[4] Literature, whether poetry, prose, or manifesto, should persist in "invoking" reality without actually getting too near it. It is "only a means … to restoring reality."[5] Even in the literature of the of *nuovo realismo,* literary language distances reader from reality, which inevitably leads to alienation.

Often, the awareness of crisis in artistic representation can be converted into the drive to find new forms of expression and new approaches to the media, and this applied particularly to the sixties. Thus Pasolini was not alone in his attitude, which he formulated in a collection of writings on language, literature, and film entitled *Empirismo eretico* (Heretical Empiricism; 1972) around that time.[6] But in contrast to the predominantly rational discourse of prestigious critics of his day, Pasolini identifies his specific problem as being the impossibility of speaking a "pure" idiom. For example, he describes how a "blue river" flows through his "Friuli poems, his finest,"[7] thereby borrowing the clothes of Romanticism. "The only [language] that can be called 'language' without qualification is the language of natural reality."[8] But unfortunately reality speaks this language only with itself, without humans being able to make use of it.[9]

Elsewhere, Pasolini describes his studio several times as a "laboratory,"[10] and the impression is created, not just in the case of *Teorema* (Theorem; 1968), of a parable-like "investigation,"[11] an experiment. The application of scientific terms to the studio and his work and the examination of an issue in various, yet parallel media, correspond to each other so closely that, contrary to references to the prevailing myth, they can be taken as clear indications of Pasolini's view toward art.

Of course, faced with the "speechless" literary avant-garde, Pasolini did not simply give it all up, but with an admirable enthusiasm and ability launched into filmmaking. Within a period of only three years (1961–1964), he produced his first independent films *Accattone, Mamma Roma, La ricotta, La rabbia, Comizi d'amore,* and *Il Vangelo secondo Matteo.* And yet his

1   Pier Paolo Pasolini, from the essay, "Who is Me," *Bestemmia: Tutte le poesie* (Milan, 1993). Marginal comments of this kind are frequent in Pasolini's notes on his work, e.g.: "With Ragazzi di vita and Una vita violenta … I placed myself in a line with Verga, Joyce, and Gadda." (*Vie Nuove* 15 [July 30, 1960], quoted in Sam Rhodie,

The Passion of Pier Paolo Pasolini [London, 1995], p. 2).

2   Pasolini, "Who is Me" (see note 1).

3   Ibid.

4   Pier Paolo Pasolini, "The End of the Avant-Garde," in *Heretical Empiricism,* trans. Ben Lawton and Louise Barnett (Bloomington, Indiana, 1988).

5   Ibid.

6   Ibid.

7   Pasolini, "Who is Me" (see note 1).

8   Pier Paolo Pasolini, "Living Signs and Dead Poets," in *Heretical Empiricism.*

9   Cf. Pasolini, "Living Signs and Dead Poets."

10   Cf. Pasolini, *Heretical Empiricism.*

literary and journalistic output flagged not a bit during this time. In fact, he threw himself into a variety of artistic activities in concert: he wrote, he drew, he made films, he was an author, actor, extra, and director. It seemed there was no aspect of art production he would not try his hand at. Though his cinematographic output may at first seem auto-didactic in many respects,[12] Pasolini was not only experienced as an author of screenplays, but by collaborating on sundry film productions had become thoroughly familiar with the processes involved in making a film.[13] Accordingly, he was able to make the switch from a literary figure to filmmaker quickly and authoritatively. Yet to his dying day, Pasolini still remained a writer as well. Indeed, in his view that was his primary artistic occupation. Even shortly before his death, when he was a celebrated director, in reply to the question what he was, he simply said *"autore"*—a statement that in turn should be seen in the context of Pasolini's view of film as a language and illustrates his transmedial perspective.

Yet, only a year after he declared his diagnosis of the "end of the avant-garde," his conversion to film seemed irreversible, and seen in isolation appears to imply a renunciation of literature: "I personally still believe in narrative cinema, i.e. I stick by the convention whereby the montage selects the important and valid sections from the endless takes that get made."[14] His confidence in film was based *inter alia* on the conviction that "pictures" are more powerful than words, which are subject to grammar, the lexicon and a determinate network of meanings: "There is no dictionary of pictures."[15] Unlike

[11] Pier Paolo Pasolini, *Teorema*, trans. Stuart Hood (London, 1992).

[12] Cf. on this point the comments by Gert Mattenklott on dilettantism as a technique in Pasolini's *Trilogia della vita:* "That probably has to do with this desperate desire to regain one's youth via the naïve, youthful, and direct, i.e. to revoke artificial means even where he controls them, and he himself knows of course at that moment that that is dilettante." Gert Mattenklott and Karsten Witte, "Kennwort 'Pasolini'. Ein Dialog," *Kraft der Vergangenheit–Zu Motiven der Filme von Pier Paolo Pasolini,* ed. Christoph Klimke (Frankfurt, 1987), p. 113.

[13] For example, *La donna del fiume,* 1954; *Il prigioniero della montagna,* 1955; *Le notti de cabiria,* 1956; *Marisa la civetta,* 1957; *Giovanni Mariti,* 1958; *La notte brava,* 1959; *Il Bell'Antonio,* 1960, etc.

[14] Pasolini, "Living Signs and Dead Poets," in *Heretical Empiricism* (see note 4), p. 245.

Pasolini filming *Mamma Roma,* 1962

writers, film directors take "their symbols … from chaos,"[16] and thus have an opportunity to make statements in a medium largely unencumbered with tradition. His second literary self-description *Una disparata vitalità* (A Desperate Vitality), which folowed "Who is Me," is Pasolini's development toward film written in a way that is typical of his approach. The first line says: "As in a film by Godard …," and is repeated three times on the first page to emphasize that the subject matter is film. It introduces a scenario wherein Pasolini imagines himself as an actor at the wheel of his Alfa Romeo—this is a citation or pastiche. In the terminology of postmodernist aesthetics, pastiches—originally a seventeenth-century painting genre—represent a kind of parody that makes use of ersatz intertextual spellings.[17] Pasolini often employs various versions of this technique. In the passage quoted here we encounter a narrative perspective reminiscent of a watchful camera; or alternatively, the depiction of his own experience reads like the description of a film scene. A component of this imagined scene is the identification (almost a travesty, in fact) of the first-person narrator and author with car-mad male stars from literature and film. These passages contain echoes of James Dean at the wheel of his Porsche and Futurist texts by Marinetti about racing cars, machismo, and danger that Pasolini had studied. In *Una disparata vitalità* for example, he writes: "I'm like a cat burnt alive, crushed by the tires of a truck,"[18] and in the introduction to the *Futurist Manifesto:* "We roared off and crushed the dogs that placed themselves under our burning tires

at the thresholds of houses."[19] Finally there appears like a fade of the picture—which Pasolini calls a citation—the name of the original protagonist, who is parodied here among others: "Belmondo, who [sits] at the wheel of his Alfa Romeo …"[20] A great number of intertextual overlays and allusions pepper this autobiographical text, in which Pasolini dramatizes his (textual) person as playing parts and wearing masks on surfaces that, because of their nature as citations and pastiches, seem fluid.

Pasolini's route to the cinema—from poetry via a novel and screenplays to storyboarding and writing, acting, and directing—already hints how different media overlap, annotate each other, and maintain complex relationships with each other synchronically and diachronically. The subject and plot of *Teorema,* Pasolini's experimental investigation of petty bourgeois ideology in Italy's *grande bourgeoise* society, were first set out in "Who is Me," continued as a screenplay and ended up as a novel and film, both of which appeared in 1968. Throughout, the plot remains simple, reminiscent of an experiment under laboratory conditions, and adheres to the first 1966 draft: a mysterious young man of extraordinary beauty is the guest of a rich family for a brief time. He sows such confusion that all the members of the household, including the maid, fall under his spell and, after he leaves, are unable to reestablish the even tenor of their lives. There is very little dialogue in either the film or the novel. The written version contains descriptions of individual plot sequences, nonverbal communications, landscapes and architecture,

---

[15] Pier Paolo Pasolini, "The Cinema of Poetry," in *Movies and Methods: An Anthology,* trans. Marianne de Vettimo and Jacques Bontemps, ed. Bill Nichols (Berkeley, 1976).

[16] Ibid.

[17] Cf. Ingeborg Hoesterey, *Pastiche: Cultural Memory in Art, Film,*

Literature (Bloomington and Indianapolis, 2001); Wolfgang Karrer, *Parodie, Travestie, Pastiche* (Munich, 1977); Wido Hempel, "Parodie, Travestie und Pastiche. Zur Geschichte von Wort und Sache," *Germanistisch-Romanisch Monatsschrift* 15 (1965), pp. 150-176.

[18] Pasolini, "Who is Me" (see note 1), p. 37.

[19] Filippo Tommaso Marinetti, "Manifest des Futurismus," *Der Sturm* 2, 104 (April 1912), p. 828-829. The parallels suggested here go further, e.g. in the descriptions of northern Italian landscapes in the introduction to the *Futurist Manifesto.*

[20] Pasolini, "Who is Me" (see note 1), p. 38

all of which parallel the film so closely that the novel almost seems to act as a screenplay.

The content of what later became *Teorema* is succinctly outlined in three pages of "Who is Me," with a distinctly ironic undertone: "The young man arrives, as beautiful as an American, and immediately the first to fall in love with him and lift her skirts is the housemaid. Then the son falls in love with him."[21] From the perspective of an observer, Pasolini jots down the plot of *Teorema* without discernible empathy for the protagonists of his story. The "cold gaze" of the camera as a technical eye and the detached attitude of the narrator are in accord. Here, too, art making and life appear intertwined inasmuch as this text also occurs in an autobiographical poem intended for publication.

In the preface to the novel, Pasolini writes about this intermedial constellation: "Developed on a gold background *Teorema* was painted with my right hand while my left hand was busy doing a fresco on a large wall … . With a dual nature of this kind, I don't know which carries more weight—the literature or the film. In truth, *Teorema* came about as a play [*pièce*] written in verse around three years earlier, which got transformed into a film and at the same time into the narrative that underlies the film and was corrected by the film."[22] Alongside this genesis of verse and film, painting and the application of a fresco are presented as artistic forms of expression and placed in a relationship with each other. The technique of frescoing is comparable to that of filming—a picture painted on fresh *intonaco* cannot be changed, any more than pictures registered on celluloid.

Pasolini describes the creative process in terms that create a distance from the specific procedure: *Teorema* "came about" and was finally "transformed" into a film. Thus a transmedial artistic process is depicted as if it were a matter of course.

Two other examples of Pasolini's experiments involving words and (photographic) pictures that are of interest in the context discussed here are *Yellowed Iconography (for a "photographic poem")* in *La Divina Mimesis* (The Divine Mimesis; 1975)[23] and *La terra vista dalla luna* (Earth Seen from the Moon; 1966)[24]. In the first, Pasolini sets up an array of black and white photos in a series that fluctuate between document and portrait, thereby placing himself in a network of reference points that nonetheless remain diffuse in their arrangement. It is a personal "yellowed iconography" that provides cursory photographic clues to the author's creed. *La terra vista dalla luna* is a storyboard and screenplay for the film of the same name and a comic in its own right.

[21] Ibid.

[22] Pasolini, *Teorema* (see note 12).

[23] Pier Paolo Pasolini, *La Divina Mimesis,* trans. Thomas Erling Peterson (Berkeley, 1980).

[24] Pier Paolo Pasolini, *Die Erde vom Mond aus gesehen–Szenario, gezeichnet* (Bolzano and Vienna, 1997).

Still from *Teorema*, 1968

Dialogues in speech bubbles and caricature drawings come together to make a humorous intermedial experiment that makes use of an aesthetic that is untypical for Pasolini. He himself considered the tragicomic search of father and son for a perfect wife and mother, rendered in garish colors, as "one of his most successful works."[25]

Sometimes it is only an undertone, sometimes it is made exaggeratedly prominent with quotation marks ("alone 'at the wheel of his Alfa Romeo,'" "a 'seven-year-old' poet, like Rimbaud") how close Pasolini is to parodying citation for all the political and moral seriousness of the parody, and how he makes use of borrowed styles and pictures. Sam Rhodie has already pointed this out: "The narrator may *write* like Proust, but it is only a likeness. The characters may *speak* like slum kids, but it is a speech corrupted by literature."[26] It almost seems as if the pastiche technique made it easier for Pasolini working across different media to switch seamlessly from

one to the next, because he always works (also) "in the style of ... ," whether it is his (self-)portraits reminiscent of Francis Bacon, his Rome novels à la Gadda, his Nietzschean tone in *La Divina Mimesis,* or his death fantasies echoing Marinetti. This phenomenon, which is also an intertextual phenomenon, is also most impressive in numerous film takes that are based on paintings.[27]

Pasolini never renounced writing despite his oft-proclaimed scepticism about literature inherent in the "invocation" of reality and written into his work as a murmuring subtext. He was looking for a form of linguistic expression and found it in the language of film—in which he worked and thought across different media: writing, drawing, and filming. It was a method that led to experiments in words and pictures in order to investigate the "phenomenology" of reality: "Cinema, which reproduces reality, i.e. becomes its 'written' language, make its essence visible and underlines its phenomenology."[28] Transmediality and pastiches are determining features of Pasolini's reality. His oeuvre is based on a creative process that employs both phenomena as techniques and exemplifies their universality.

Still from *La terra vista dalla luna,* 1966

[25] *Pasolini su Pasolini. Conversazioni con Jon Halliday* (Parma, 1992).

[26] Rhodie (see note 1) p. 2.

[27] Cf. Alberto Marchesini, *Citazioni pittoriche nel cinema di Pasolini (da Accattone al Decameron),* Florence 1994; Günter Minas, "'Ein Fresko auf einer grossen Wand ...'—Die Bedeutung der Malerei für die Filmarbeit Pasolinis," *Kraft der Vergangenheit—Zu Motiven der Filme von Pier Paolo Pasolini,* ed. Christoph Klimke (Frankfurt, 1987), pp. 51–69. With regard to Pasolini's films, Minas speaks of recognizable "stylistic similarities," which more or less corresponds to the term pastiche as understood here (cf. ibid., p. 55).

[28] Pasolini, "The End of the Avant-Garde."

From the storyboard of *La terra
vista dalla luna*, 1966

Benjamin Meyer-Krahmer *is a literary scholar, curator,
and scenographer in Berlin. He has contributed to a number
of publications on contemporary art.*

P.P.P.

PIER PAOLO PASOLINI

Popular
Paradox
Poetic

Preceding page
Pasolini drawing, c. 1970

A Dialect of the "Language of Poetry"

On the Drawings of Pier Paolo Pasolini
Michael Semff

Pasolini's artwork was still largely unknown a quarter century ago, when it was introduced to the public through exhibitions and publications. For many this was an exciting new encounter with one of the most multi-faceted artists of the second half of the twentieth century.[1]

Several hundred of his drawings have still exist.[2] Clearly, drawing was one of the most inspired—and most inspiring—pursuits for Pasolini during certain periods of his life, including his early years in Friuli and also his time in Rome starting in the 1960s, when he was dedicating most of his energy to film. The fact that Pasolini did not produce any drawings between 1950 and 1965 (with the exception of two with definitive dates)[3] is due mostly to the difficult circumstances he faced after his move from Casarsa to Rome in late 1949. He spent these years establishing a new existence, one in which his literary pursuits largely took precedence.

As a rule Pasolini's drawings are not really those of a film director. Only a very few serve as a means of developing concrete visual concepts for a final film. Extended series of drawings, such as the thirty-four sheets of *La terra vista dalla luna* from 1966 (a kind of comic series serving as a "sketched screenplay" for the first part of this episode film) are the rarest exceptions.[4] The direct relationship between drawings and cinematic work has parallels with the drawings of Federico Fellini, a friend of Pasolini's from mid-fifties on. Noticeable here is a pronounced tendency towards drastic extremes and grotesque exaggeration in his characters, the characteristic humor in the intensity of faces and figurative scenarios that was the hallmark of Fellini's draftsmanship. Like Fellini, Pasolini needed to give his overflowing imagination an outlet through drawing. However, the majority of Pasolini's drawings—despite their fragile, sketchy, and even fragmented appearance—are characterized by a completely different syntax. They are almost exclu-

sively independent compositions on individual sheets of paper. Both the breadth of expression and the varying mentality of drawing, which are largely the result of the media employed, reveal a hidden, and thus all the more powerful, facet of Pasolini that enriches our picture of the artist. As a draftsman Pasolini chose fairly conventional imagery for his subject matter: portraits, self-portraits, figural studies, landscapes, and animals. His iconographic repertoire never contains anything offensive or scandalous. One will search in vain for pointed sexual or homoerotic motifs familiar in the work of de Pisis, for example.

In an essay from over twenty years ago that would be difficult to better, Helmut Heissenbüttel made it clear that one should be careful about describing Pasolini as "doubly gifted."[5] Varying from case to case, it is the random whim of individual interpreters of his work

---

The title of this essay is based on a note in Pier Paolo Pasolini's papers (c. 1970), quoted from Reiter and Zigaina 1982 (see note1), p. 7.

[1] Giuseppe Zigaina, *Pier Paolo Pasolini, I disgni 1941–1975* (Milan, 1978), and Johannes Reiter and Giuseppe Zigaina, *Pier Paolo Pasolini – Zeichnungen und Gemälde* (Basel, 1982).

[2] The majority of the drawings are held in the Gabinetto Scientifico Letterario G.P. Vieusseux, Florence.

[3] This includes a drawing *Paolo* from 1950 and a self-portrait from 1954; see Reiter and Zigaina 1982 (see note 1), plates 55, 78.

[4] Ibid., plates 87–120.

[5] Helmut Heissenbüttel, "Zeichnung als Ketzerei," in Reiter and Zigaina 1982 (see note 1), pp. 15–18.

From the storyboard of *La terra vista dalla luna*, 1966

who decide which of Pasolini's chosen media were truly dominant and which were minor. His drawings, and the glowing intensity they emit, reinforce the impression that the act of drawing was all consuming for Pasolini. His drawings are by no means marginal diversions from his usual spectrum of creative work. They are on equal footing with his other creative pursuits, the intimate expression of a highly sensitive subject. With their immediacy and private nature, which from the very start exclude any consideration of an audience, Pasolini's drawings touch on a realm of lyrical tenderness and personal feeling that hardly any other medium could communicate with such directness.

For Pasolini, originally faced with the question whether he should professionally develop his talent for painting and drawing, the ingenuousness of drawing must have served as a means of relaxation throughout his life. He could breathe freely while drawing, without an apparent purpose, without being bound by limitations or commissions. Because he was fully immersed in this activity, deep within his most intimate thoughts, the drawings are deeply marked by integrity, honesty, and even nakedness, which are never threatened by the danger of posturing. Expressed in Pasolini's drawings is evidence of his "unmistakable identity" in something that goes "beyond all ... differentiation."[6] Pasolini "is so unequivocally present in many of his drawings, in a way that an artist producing art could never achieve."[7]

The following is intended to illustrate the typical characteristics of Pasolni's drawings with the help of a few particular examples, but without art historical cat-egorization. The majority of his "trial and error experiments"[8] reveal the "indefinite, agile quality of drawing," for which "the vaguest descriptions are the most precise."[9] Among his earliest works is a group of portraits done on cellophane, which specifically call to mind the "translated" and somehow "indirect" immediacy of monotypes. One of the most powerful is the small sheet titled *Ragazzo* (Boy; ill.1, p. 130) from 1943 that captures the face of a boy in front of a horizontal "barrier." Barely larger than the width of a hand, it conveys a sense of an intensified present moment, which has been achieved through the sweeping gesture of the oil paint—marked by trace indentations made with the brush handle. Through the forms of the face, the thick, curly hair, and the frontal gaze of the eyes, rendered with a few sparing strokes, this presence gains a dimensionality that has the feeling of a frozen moment, a film still from an endless sequence of moving images. Pasolini specifically touched on this kind of work in recordings dating from around 1970: "Even thirty years ago I created problems for myself with the material. I did most of the drawings from this period on cellophane by smearing the tip of my finger with color directly from the tube, or I drew directly with the tube of paint by pressing it out ... One can't say, though, that I am a 'material painter' (or that I maybe still am). I am more interested in the 'composition'—and its contours—than the material. But I am only able to achieve the forms I want with the contours I want when the material is unwieldy, or even impossible, and they turn out best when the material is 'valuable' in some way."[10] Pasolini's

---

[6] Ibid., p. 16.

[7] Ibid.

[8] Ibid., p. 17.

[9] Karl Bohrmann, *Notizen 1972–1986* (Frankfurt am Main, 1988), p. 47, 65.

[10] Reiter and Zigaina 1982 (see note 1), p. 7.

"problems … with the material" and the experimental nature of his "trial and error experiments" in no way contradict the fact that the subject matter of these works seems so thoroughly traditional. In fact, this is something that the artist greatly emphasized in reflection on his later work: "Just as in 1943, today the themes of my paintings are also simply familiar, ordinary, tender, and definitely idyllic in nature."[11] In retrospect, the resemblance of the cellophane he used to the transparent quality of film is compelling evidence of inherent interrelationships in his work. It is no coincidence that the idea of drawing on a transparent surface reappears in a scene in *Teorema* (1968). Pietro, the homosexual son of the family—an artist searching for his own identity and thereby a possible self-portrait of the director himself[12]—tries out various painting surfaces "that reveal a view of the shifting reality in the background, which is incorporated into the image."[13] He is searching for an encounter with the infinitely more expressive power of reality. As a pictorial medium the film is both a forward-looking projection and a transparent look back. All of the traces left on the film have something perplexingly ephemeral; an ambivalence analogous to the metaphors of water and reflection (as with Narcissus: a painful recognition of the self in the mirrored image) that have fundamental significance in Pasolini's work. Another example of the creative exchange between different elements inherent in an artistic oeuvre is the obvious relationship between the transparent effect of Sigmar Polke's watercolor brushwork and the effect of paint on glass. The resemblance is all the more convinc-

ing given that, in his early years, the artist was professionally trained in glasswork.[14]

In addition to the oil sketches, a great deal of what has been handed down to us includes ink drawings dating through the end of the forties. Generally carried out on very thin paper, these are also characterized by convention. Pasolini also used pencil and, less often, tempera and pastel. Beginning in the mid-sixties, the second phase of his works on paper, was dominated by experimental mixed media and colored chalk. Some of the most delicate and fragile works of his entire oeuvre stem from the pure ink drawings of his early years. One example, from 1942, shows both male and female figures in pastoral settings, on the water, or on a ship; the figures are shown in lost dreamy reverie or playing with a frog on the shore. The brittle, even scratchy line of the gossamer-thin quill is applied without any maneuvering adjustments and calls to mind Alfred Kubin, and a number of drawings by Giuseppe Diamantini in an older Venetian context.[15] This use of line effects a highly unique expression of reticent lyricism in these narrative "allegories." The language of the unusual *Ragazza di San Vito* (Girl from San Vito), drawn a year later, is completely different. The girl's facial features are classic and even. Reminiscent of Picasso, the portrait invokes the typology of the ancient *herme*. The face seems to grow out of a vase, and Pasolini treats the rich shock of hair much like the leafy, floral framing of a bouquets. We become aware of a shy and tender attempt at idealized femininity, which also functions as a statue-like memorial. The mortal world and Eros do not hold sway

[11] Ibid., pp. 7–8.

[12] Marc Gervais, *Pier Paolo Pasolini* (Paris, 1973), p. 82.

[13] Günter Minas, "'Ein Fresko auf einer großen Wand …' Die Bedeutung der Malerei für die Filmarbeit Pasolinis," *Kraft der Vergangenheit—Zu Motiven der Filme von Pier Paolo Pasolini* (Frankfurt am Main, 1987), p. 63.

[14] See Michael Semff, "Linie, Raster und Glasmalerei auf Papier. Beobachtungen zu artistischen Prinzipien des Zeichners Sigmar Polke," *Sigmar Polke, Arbeiten auf Papier 1963–1974*, exh. cat. Hamburger Kunsthalle (Ostfildern-Ruit, 1999), pp. 23–30.

[15] Cf *Italienische Zeichnungen 1500–1800*, ed. Christel Thiem, exh. cat. Staatsgalerie Stuttgart (Stuttgart, 1977), pp. 139–148.

in this image; instead there is an aura of the "elect and mysterious."[16] Under the spell of such magical works one grasps a sense of Pasolini's elusive description of his so-called "dialectical" painting, which he termed as "material for the tabernacle" in which he sensed the "light of things."[17]

Pasolini made a few ink landscape drawings, a theme he ordinarily reserved for his paintings. The landscapes take the form of light notations evoking a spontaneously recorded observation *(La casa crollata,* The Destroyed House; 1943) or sketches that also unfold as powerful drawings, as in the work *Paesaggio di Casarsa* (Landscape near Casarsa) from the same year. Here, a broad, gentle, and rhythmic stroke of the pen uniformly captures forms that are then drawn into an autonomous graphic texture. The panel format drawing *Meriggi sul prato* (Midday on the Meadow) almost seems to be a direct homage to Giorgio Morandi. The drawing bears a poem of five lines that has a similar tone to the evocative nature poetry of Giacomo Leopardi, one of Morandi's favorite poets. The motif and line of the pen in the drawing from 1943 seem to directly echo the barren landscapes that Morandi produced in Grizzana, also during the war.[18] Two extreme, large-format landscape works in mixed media are worthy of note and, unusual for Pasolini, they border on abstraction. *Barene col cielo grigio* (Sandbank Beneath a Grey Sky; 1969) is one example.[19] One is a monochrome, sand-colored expanse that is defined only by a few sparing hints of horizontal line and shows an almost imperceptible hint of shading on the horizon. The other (ill. p. 144) is animated by

[16] Reiter and Zigaina 1982 (see note 1), p. 8.

[17] Ibid.

[18] The ink drawings mentioned are depicted in: Reiter and Zigaina, 1982, plates 29, 31, 28. For the comparison with Morandi see: Michael Semff, "Die Entrückung der Nähe, über die letzten Zeichnungen Giorgio Morandi," in *Giorgio Morandi: Die letzten Zeichnungen,* exh. cat. Staatliche Graphische Sammlung München (Munich, 2000), pp. 20ff.

[19] Reiter and Zigaina 1982 (see note 1), nos. 77 and 78.

Girl from San Vito, 1943
Pen and ink on paper,
15 x 17.5 cm
Gabinetto Scientifico Letterario
G. P. Vieusseux, Florence

a murky form placed horizontally in the center of the image so that it almost functions like collage. Even if it goes against the explicit intentions of the artist, who vehemently defended figuration and railed against the formalistic tendencies of abstraction and informal art,[20] one could legitimately sense an urge to draw parallels with works by Cy Twombly (for example, his picture *Untitled* from the same year) or some of Jean Fautrier's work.

Although Pasolini tried a number of unusual techniques beginning in the forties, his impulse to experiment, an act almost bordering on alchemy, was noticeably heightened in his works on paper dating from the last ten years of his life. In the [Maria] Callas portraits (ills. pp. 126, 138, 139) produced during the filming of *Medea* in 1969/70 he forced an encounter between absolutely incompatible materials, and the interaction on the surface of the paper lead to utterly unpredictable results. Due to his very close relationship to the legendary diva, he was under great mental strain during these months. His obsessive pursuit of the secret of her being and his vision of transcending her myth seemed achievable through the use of pastiche, which he began to discuss openly in 1946.[21] In the context of his linguistic research Pasolini made emphatic references to the predominant stylistic device of "contamination" (expressed most effectively in the later Callas portraits), which helped him in his attempts to express "nature with nature" and "reality with reality" through what seemed to be utter contradictions.[22] These are either individual sheets or tableau-like rows of portraits, much like a roll of film negative, that show Maria Callas mostly in profile and in almost identical poses. A spotty layer of natural tones carpets all the sheets; it seems to eat into the paper like an acid disfiguring or even dissolving the rhythm of individual forms to the point that they merely appear as flickering traces of something that is no more. These represent both extraordinary attempts at remembering and the banishment of the human subject matter at the same time. With these drawings Pasolini created relics of something about to disappear, the transitory moment of crossing from one state to another, in which life, dissolution, and even "deliverance,"[23] the instant of presence and passing, palpably hang in the air. To add another observation, Pasolini usually shows Callas in profile with open eyes, but in a few drawings, and not incidentally in the same pose, with her eyes closed. This expression of artistic exaltation matched with conceptual stringency makes this series a highpoint in Pasolini's legacy of drawings. In contrast, the self-portraits from 1965 (ills. pp. 136–137) more closely adhere to the practices of the portrait tradition, despite the penetrating psychological questioning of the opposing self and the casual treatment of the largely frontal gaze that is intensely fixed on the viewer. Finally, the profiles of his much-adored teacher Roberto Longhi (ills. p. 61) produced in Chia shortly before Pasolini's death, display a style that is not so far from caricature, with their broad abbreviations of line. Despite his tendency to dissolve or transform facial features into almost abstract compositions, these drawings lack the spirituality and animistic magic found

---

[20] See Laura Safred, "Unzeitgemäße Bilder–Pasolini und die visuelle Kunst," *Pier Paolo Pasolini oder die Grenzüberschreitung–organizzar il trasumanar* (Venice, 1995), p. 185.

[21] According to Giuseppe Zigaina, "Das Zeichen, unter dem ich arbeite, ist die Kontamination," in Reiter and Zigaina 1982, p. 29.

[22] Otto Schweitzer, *Pier Paolo Pasolini* (Reinbek bei Hamburg, 2000), p. 33.

[23] Ibid., pp. 107–108.

in Callas' majestic profile and in the portraits of artist friends Andrea Zanzotto and Giuseppe Zigaina. Pasolini the poet reaffirmed the phenomenon of vivid Pontormo-esque colors within the immediacy of life, and out of a stream of emotion and tenderness came the mystery that emerges a few years later in works like the Callas portraits.[24] While he spoke of "color" and "sheen," of "the poppies … on a melancholy afternoon in the embers of a cemetery," of "papery pale" and the "living red," of "empty space" and "nothingness," of "something that was once red and is now a sweet-scented shadow," no words are needed to conjure the "revivifying enchantment of alchemy"[25] that makes the Callas portraits so unique.

To conclude these observations, let us consider an unusual drawing with the inscription: *Il mondo non mi vuole più e non lo sa* (The world does not want me any more and does not know it; ills. pp. 142, 143) that seems to openly announce a life crisis. There has been much speculation about this puzzling drawing,[26] which cannot be clearly dated. Was does the sequence of the four-by-four array of shapes—placed one over the other, uniformly diagonal—indicate? Do these symbols, each one slightly modified, refer to anything specific?[27] They are an arrangement of criss-crossing straight lines, each one nearing a single organic and discharging line. Usually both formal realms touch or interrupt each other. Here, no definitive new interpretation of this mysterious drawing can be offered. However, in this context a reading of Pasolini's later poems is revealing; one example is the edited volume *Trasumanar e organizzar* from

---

Working on the Maria Callas portraits on the Greek island of Skorpios, August 1970

[24] Pier Paolo Pasolini, *Alì dagli occhi azzurri* (Milan, 1965), according to Mario de Micheli, "Die mystisch-naturalistischen Inspirationen des Malers Pier Paolo Pasolini," Reiter and Zigaina 1982, pp. 21–22.

[25] Giuseppe Zigaina, "Das Zeichen, unter dem ich arbeite, ist die Kontamination," in Reiter and Zigaina 1982, p. 30.

[26] For example, see Mario de Micheli, in Reiter and Zigaina 1982, p. 23; Giuseppe Zigaina, ibid., p. 31; and Christoph Meckel, "Der Zeichner Pasolini," ibid., p. 56.

[27] Mario de Micheli's adamant interpretation of these as the artist's words is quite difficult to follow. See Mario de Micheli, in Reiter and Zigaina 1982, p. 23.

Portrait of Maria Callas, 1969
Mixed technique on paper,
24.4 x 32.5 cm
Private collection

1971 based on the *cantus firmus* of his hopeless love for Callas. Revealed in this volume, Pasolini's "inability to want poetry,"[28] his recognition of the "meaninglessness of every word"[29] aptly corresponds to the intentional emptiness in the composition of the drawing with its "almost mechanical representation of an obsessive idea", a kind of "graphic trace of the seismograph indicating a disruption of balance."[30] Schweitzer's interpretation of the poems evokes the essence of this drawing—one that stands out so prominently from the rest of his oeuvre: "Stillness, emptiness is the underlying message of these poems. Their form, the destruction of form, is an expression of his defeat and his distance to what was happening around him. Leaving art is an expression of leaving reality, which he, the heretic, had already left behind, and reality had abandoned him: he is no longer needed."[31] He is no longer desired …

---

[28] Schweitzer 2000 (see note 22), p. 109.

[29] See Pasolini's poem "Il gracco," in *Trasumanar e organizzar* (Milan, 1971), p. 51.

[30] Giuseppe Zigaina, in Reiter and Zigaina 1982, p. 31. Given these considerations, Zigaina's dating of the drawing "around 1972" (according to the technique employed) seems even more plausible.

[31] Schweitzer 2000 (see note 22), pp. 109–110.

Michael Semff *is director of the Staatliche Graphische Sammlung in Munich.*

1

2

Preceding page
**Seated Figure in a Landscape,
undated**
Pen and chalk on paper,
33.5 x 23.5 cm
Gabinetto Scientifico Letterario
G. P. Vieusseux, Florence

1 Boy, undated (1943)
Oil on cellophane,
14 x 12.5 cm
Gabinetto Scientifico Letterario
G. P. Vieusseux, Florence

2 Boy Sitting in Bed, 1943
Oil on cellophane,
14.8 x 13 cm
Gabinetto Scientifico Letterario
G. P. Vieusseux, Florence

3 Boy, undated (1943)
Oil on cellophane,
18.2 x 13 cm
Gabinetto Scientifico Letterario
G. P. Vieusseux, Florence

3

4

4 Seated Boy, 1943
  Pen and ink on paper,
  20.5 x 15 cm
  Gabinetto Scientifico Letterario
  G. P. Vieusseux, Florence

5 Three Seated Mountain Soldiers,
  1942
  Pen and ink on typing paper,
  12.2 x 21 cm
  Gabinetto Scientifico Letterario
  G. P. Vieusseux, Florence

5

1

2

3

4

5

1, 2 Mountains Behind Trees
(verso)/Degradare di monti
(recto), undated
Pen and ink on paper,
16.3 x 24 cm
Gabinetto Scientifico Letterario
G. P. Vieusseux, Florence

3 Landscape Near Casarsa, 1944
Oil on canvas,
46.5 x 55 cm
Private collection

4 Vase of Flowers, undated
Oil on paper,
29.6 x 24.8 cm
Gabinetto Scientifico Letterario
G. P. Vieusseux, Florence

5 Narcissus, 1947
Tempera and pastel on brown
paper, 27 x 37 cm
Gabinetto Scientifico Letterario
G. P. Vieusseux, Florence

134

1

1 **Self-Portrait with Old Scarf, 1946**
  Tempera on hardboard,
  42.8 x 38 cm
  Gabinetto Scientifico Letterario
  G. P. Vieusseux, Florence

2 **Self-Portrait, 1947**
  Tempera on hardboard,
  42.5 x 34.5 cm
  Gabinetto Scientifico Letterario
  G. P. Vieusseux, Florence

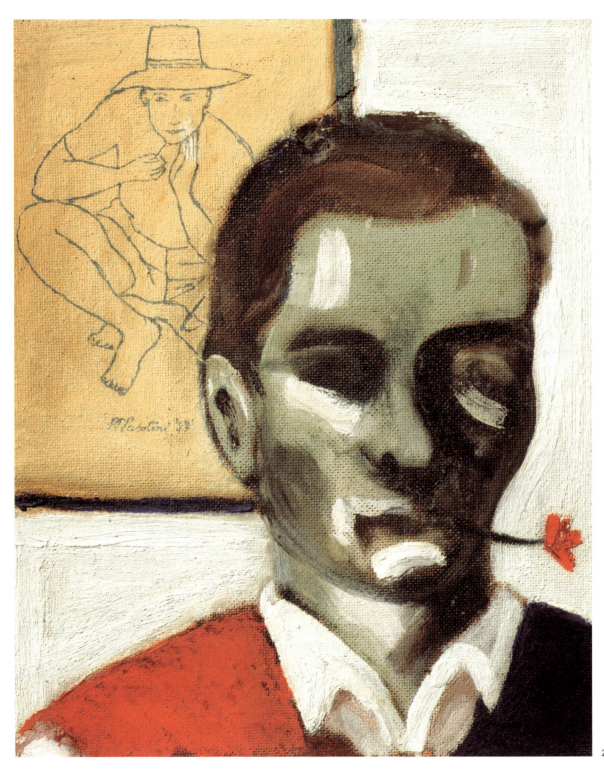

2

2

1

3

Preceding page
Self-Portrait, 1965
Colored pen on paper,
32.6 x 24.4 cm
Gabinetto Scientifico Letterario
G. P. Vieusseux, Florence

1 **Self-Portrait,** 1965
Pen on paper,
32.6 x 24.4 cm
Gabinetto Scientifico Letterario
G. P. Vieusseux, Florence

2 **Self-Portrait,** 1965
Ocher colored pen on paper,
32.6 x 24.4 cm
Gabinetto Scientifico Letterario
G. P. Vieusseux, Florence

3 **Self-Portrait,** 1965
Ocher colored pen on paper,
32.6 x 24.4 cm
Gabinetto Scientifico Letterario
G. P. Vieusseux, Florence

1

2

3

1 Portrait of Maria Callas, 1969
Mixed technique on paper,
70 x 50.4 cm
Private collection

2 Portrait of Maria Callas, 1969
Mixed technique on paper,
70 x 49.7 cm
Private collection

3 Portrait of Maria Callas, 1969
Mixed technique on paper,
32.3 x 34.9 cm
Private collection

Opposite
Portraits of Maria Callas, 1970
Mixed technique on paper,
73 x 51 cm
Gabinetto Scientifico Letterario
G. P. Vieusseux, Florence

Poles and Nets on Safon, 1970
Mixed technique on paper,
41 x 31.1 cm
Private collection

1

2

3

4

1 Portrait of Andrea Zanzotto, 1974
  Oil and woodstain on paper,
  49.8 x 37.9 cm
  Private collection

2 Portrait of Andrea Zanzotto, 1974
  Mixed technique on paper,
  47.5 x 31 cm
  Private collection

3 Portrait of Andrea Zanzotto, 1974
  Mixed technique on paper,
  25 x 32.5 cm
  Private collection

4 Portrait of Andrea Zanzotto, 1974
  Graese pencil on paper,
  31.7 x 29 cm
  Private collection

Il mondo non mi vuole
più e non lo sa

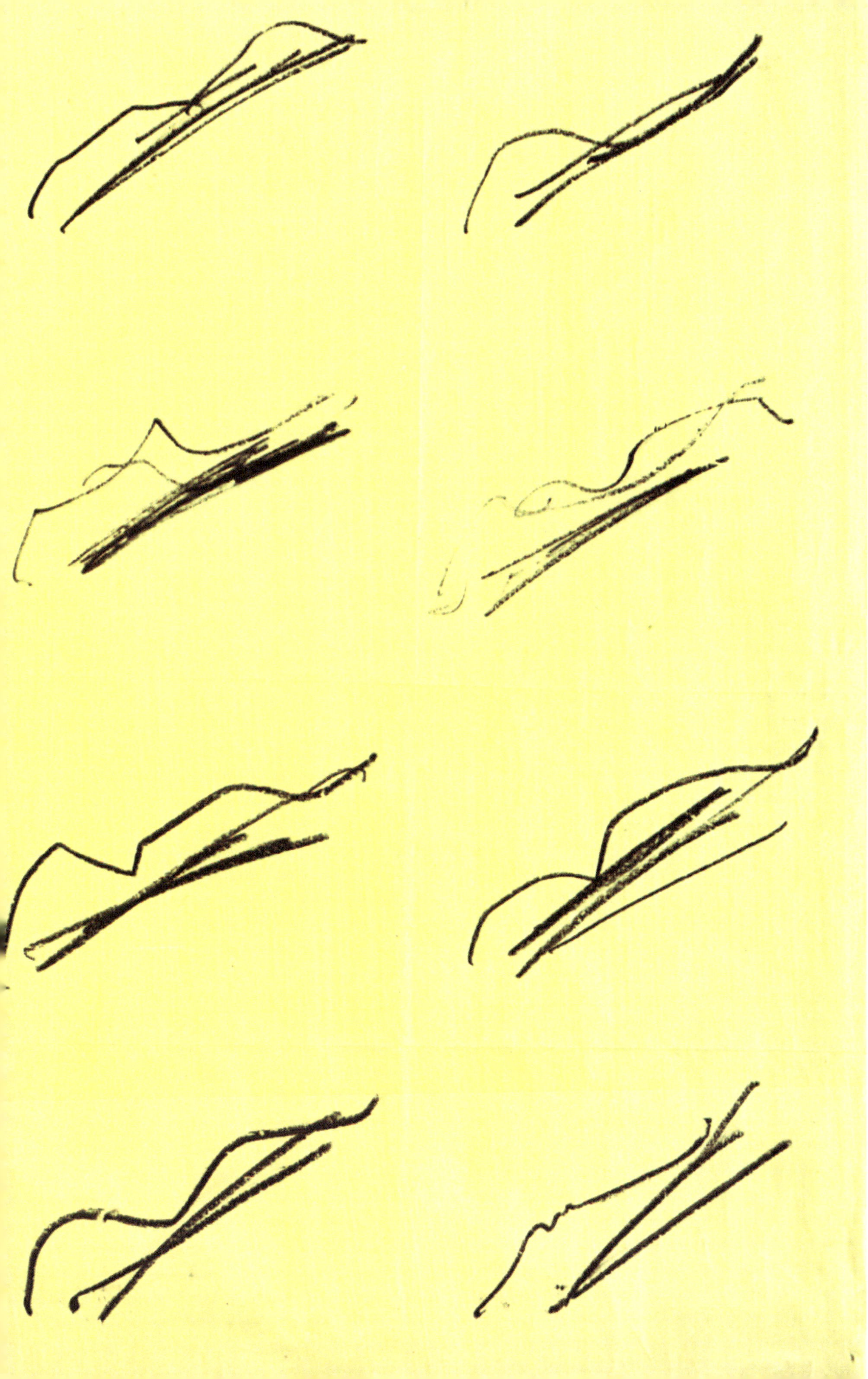

Sandbanks Beneath a Gray Sky, 1969
Mixed technique on paper,
50 x 70 cm
Private collection

Preceding page
"Il mondo non mi vuole più e non lo sa"
(The world doesn't want me any more
and doesn't know it), undated
Charcoal on yellow paper,
52 x 65 cm
Gabinetto Scientifico Letterario
G. P. Vieusseux, Florence

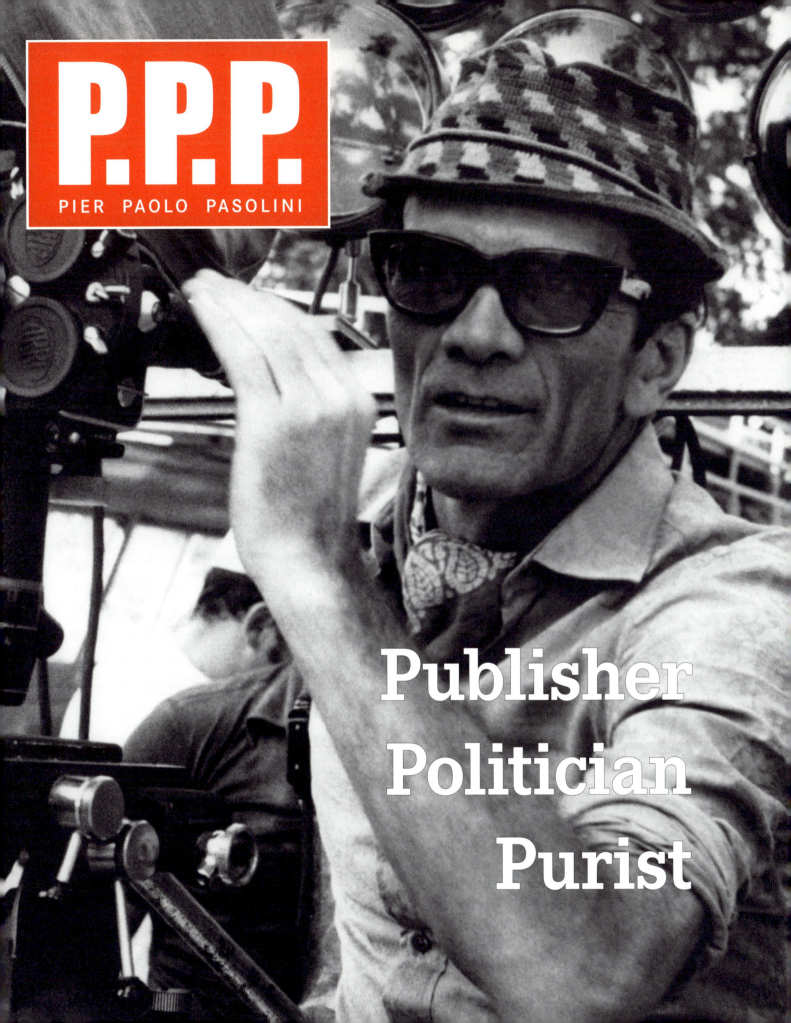

P.P.P.

PIER PAOLO PASOLINI

Publisher
Politician
Purist

Preceding page
Pasolini filming the *Arabian Nights*, 1973

Patmos

Pier Paolo Pasolini

Patmos was written during the night of December 13–14, 1969, in the aftermath of the bomb attack on the Banca Nazionale dell'Agricoltura in Milan, the first major terrorist attack in Italy since World War II. The comments are by the author.

The editors have chosen to reprint the original Italian version (first published in *Nuovi argomenti,* in December of that year) of the poem to illustrate Pasolini's true intention with tone, wording, and structure.

Sono sotto choc
è giunto fino a Patmos sentore
di ciò che annusano i cappellani
i morti erano tutti dai cinquanta ai settanta
la mia età fra pochi anni, rivelazione di Gesù Cristo
che Dio, per istruire i suoi servi
—sulle cose che devono ben presto accadere—
ha fatto conoscere per mezzo del suo Angelo
al proprio servo Giovanni.
Ci sono là marcite; e molti pioppi. Venendo da là
vestivano di grigio e marrone; la roba pesante,
che fuma nelle osterie con le latrine all'aperto.
Poca creanza, farsi ritrovare così,
da parte di quei galantuomini non ancora del tutto romanizzati,
e sì che tutti i barocci erano spariti da un pezzo!
Ma gli usati corpi, non di monaci,
perché cattolici erano cattolici, ma s'erano sposati, fornicando
la loro parte; insomma, giusto perché dei nipotini oggi piangessero.
Solo un suicidio porterà sulle tracce del responsabile di tal pianto.[1]
Lombardi al Governo! Tra voi e il paese c'è un abisso.
È la vostra banalità che lo scava (le "e" strette
son niente confronto al lessico; che umile dialetto non è;
lo fosse!)
E chi è sotto choc ride con gli occhi di Antonioni
Il quale attesta come parola di Dio e testimonianza di Gesù Cristo
e anche Pasolini ride,
tutto quello che ha veduto,
mentre Moravia è distratto, beato chi legge,
e beati coloro che ascoltano le parole di questa profezia.
Che ne piangano le loro famiglie; io ne parlo da letterato.
Oppongo al cordoglio un certo manierismo.
Di tradizioni recenti son piene le Sette Chiesuole.
Canoni e tropi a disposizione rimpiazzano le commozioni;
e basta deciderlo, l'umore necessario è pronto
con tutti i suoi caratteri

---

[1] Questi versi sono stati scritti
tra il 13 e il 14 dicembre;
prima che si sapesse del suicidio dell'anarchico Pinelli.

(di difesa dietro il lessico, esso, eslege, desueto)
chi è al potere altresì ha le sue figure
entro cui comodamente sostituire al logos il nulla;
dietro una cattedra, un tavolo da lavoro,
col doppiopetto: perché il tempo è lontano.
Così si consola la morte, e chi ha la cattiva creanza
di farsi piangere; ridotto a tronconi: cosa inammissibile
in un uomo serio, che si occupa di agricoltura!
Come poi se fossimo nel '44.
Io sono l'Alfa e l'Omega, colui che è, che era e che viene; l'Onnipotente;
fidando su ciò, l'onorevole Rumor, Pocopotente
ma Potente, comunque,
si dissocia dai telespettatori dei bar
e parla ai piccoli borghesi in famiglia che si saziano
di indignazione del tutto lessicalmente estranea al popolo.
Attilio Valè: presente!
52 anni, abitava a Mairano di Noviglio.
Era separato da otto anni dalla moglie;
era un bell'uomo alto circa un metro e ottanta:
commerciava in bestiame
Io, Giovanni, vostro fratello,
che partecipa con voi alla stessa tribolazione
al regno e alla perseveranza di Gesù,
mi trovai relegato nell'isola chiamata Patmos
a causa del Vangelo di Dio e delle testimonianze che rendevo a Gesù.
L'Autorità dello Stato moderato non contempla la realtà dei sensali.
Pietro Dendena (presente!) 45 anni,
abitava a Lodi in un nuovo edificio di Via Italia 11
con la moglie Luisa Corbellini, la figlia Franca, 17 anni,
che frequenta il corso di segretariato d'azienda,
e il figlio Paolo, 10 anni, alunno di quinta elementare.
Di professione mediatore,
frequentava regolarmente il mercato di Piazza Fontana
non mi meraviglierei da letterato schizoide
che comparisse tale e quale in un olio del Prado

né che avesse un debole per l'Inter;
ci son portichetti a Lodi, tetramente settentrionali—
contro un cielo buio, con nuvole basse—
micragna dei tempi degli Antenati, odor di vacche!
Lè il dì di mort (tutti presenti).
Quanto a Paolo Gerli, 77 anni (presente)
ci son portichetti a Lodi a sesto acuto,
e le piccole osterie micragnose sanno di vestiti bagnati
riscaldati dalla stufa
abitava con la moglie in un bellissimo palazzo di Via Savaré, 1,
dove si era trasferito nel 1954
possidente di non pochi terreni agricoli,
curava in proprio il commercio dei prodotti della sua terra.
I vicini di casa, loro,
lo ricordano come un signore gioviale e esuberante.
Usava regolarmente la bicicletta.
Aveva avuto dal matrimonio tre figlie tutte sposate.
Or, ecco, fui rapito in estasi, nel giorno del Signore
e udii dietro a me una voce potente, come di tromba
Eugenio Corsini, 55 anni, presente!
abitava dall'epoca delle nozze in Via Procopio 8,
padre di due figli ormai sposati,
commerciava in olii lubrificanti per macchine agricole.
La moglie non aveva smesso di lavorare.
Non si cantarono serenate in quel 1940;
dal 1940 si era lavorato giudiziosamente, a casa a far la calza.
Si erano frequentate scuole in vista di futuri risparmi;
niente grilli per la testa, che nessuno avesse niente da ridire;
la Morale come una cosa passata di donna in donna;
poco riso negli occhi, e gran risate al momento giusto: a Natale.
Io mi voltai per vedere la voce che parlava
e appena voltato vidi sette candelabri d'oro
Carlo Luigi Perego, 74 anni, risiedeva a Usmate Velate
e in mezzo ai candelabri Uno che assomigliava al Figlio dell'Uomo
in Via Stazione 21

vestito di una lunga veste
lascia la moglie e due figli sposati
che hanno proseguito la sua attività di assicuratore
e cinto d'una fascia d'oro sul petto
Era venuto a Milano per rivedere i vecchi amici
e per sbrigare alcune faccende relative all'attività dei figli
Il suo capo e i suoi capelli erano bianchi come lana
i suoi piedi erano simili a rame ardente arroventato in una fornace
(così disse chi li raccolse sotto il bancone)
Aveva presieduto, in qualità di coraggioso combattente del '15–18
la locale sezione dell'associazione dei combattenti. Presente!
Carlo Garavaglia, 67 anni, presente!
Alla morte della moglie era andato a abitare con la figlia sposata
la sua voce era come il rumore delle grandi acque
a Corsico in Via XX Settembre 19.
Nella destra teneva sette stelle.
Era stato macellaio
dalla sua bocca usciva un'acuta spada a due tagli
percepiva attualmente una pensione di 18 mila lire.
La sua faccia era come il sole.
Tentava di realizzare qualche guadagno extra facendo il mediatore.
Carlo Gaiani, presente, 57 anni,
abitava con la moglie alla cascina Salesiana
Era perito agrario
ed aveva condotto con successo l'azienda agricola
che conduceva come affittuario, fino ad alcuni anni addietro.
Ora l'azienda era in decadenza.
Lavorava personalmente la terra con un solo lavorante.
Si era recato alla Banca dell'Agricoltura
per concludere la vendita delle ultime 14 vacche.
Saragat taccio, ma ne parla l'"Observer." [2]
Oreste Sangalli, 49 anni: "Presente!"
affittuario della cascina Ronchetto in via Merula 13 a Milano
mettiamo la sordina alla tromba di quell'Uno
lascia la moglie e due ragazzi, Franco di 13 e Claudio di 11

[2] Ricordo di nuovo al lettore che
questi versi sono stati scritti solo il
giorno dopo i fatti di cui si parla.

fare d'ogni erba un fascio degli estremisti
si era recato al mercato di Piazza Fontana
va bene per i giornali indipendenti (dalla Verità)
come tutti i venerdì in compagnia di Luigi Meloni
ma un presidente della Repubblica!
Si erano momentaneamente lasciati a Porta Ticinese
Non si può predicare moderazione
e si erano dati appuntamento a Piazza Fontana
in un paese dove è appunto la moderazione che va male
Hanno trovato entrambi la morte
e dove non si può essere moderati senza essere banali
poco dopo essersi ritrovati.
Luigi Meloni, 57 anni presente:
commerciante di bestiame abitava a Corsico in Via Cavour
con la moglie e il figlio Mario, studente di 18 anni.
Possiede qualche piccola proprietà immobiliare.
Era venuto a Milano con la vettura del Sangalli.
E quando l'ebbi veduto io caddi ai suoi piedi come morto.
Ma egli pose sopra di me la sua destra e disse:
Non temere, io sono il Primo e l'Ultimo.
Io sono il Medio, parvero dire Rumor e i suoi colleghi.
Non si può essere medi, qui, senza essere privi d'immaginazione.
Io sono il Primo e l'Ultimo, il Vivente.
Giulio China, 57 anni, presente!!
Era uno dei più importanti commercianti di bestiame di Novara,
ove possedeva due cascine. Lascia la moglie e due figlie sposate.
Ho subìto la morte, ma ecco, ora vivo nei secoli dei secoli
(a differenza di Giulio China)
e tengo le chiavi della morte e dell'inferno.
Mario Pasi, cinquant'anni: presente,
abitava con la moglie in un bell'appartamento di Via Mercalli 16.
Ah antichi portichetti a sesto acuto, grigi, scrostati,
sotto cui l'ombra è così fredda che par di essere in Germania
e i negozietti di mercerie stringono il cuore, e ancor più
se vi si vendono anche caramelle, in scatole di cartone

Ma ci son anche palazzi di metallo e vetro
che danno sui parchi
Non aveva figli. Geometra,
si era dedicato all' amministrazione di fondi e stabili.
Era stato ufficiale di cavalleria.
Scrivi dunque le cose che hai vedute,
e le presenti e quelle che verranno dopo di esse:
l'Italia è in crisi, e la stessa crisi che soffro io
(inadattabilità alle nuove operazioni bancarie)
la soffrono alla loro bestial maniera i fascisti:
le ultime 14 vacche! Le ultime 14 vacche!
Ecco il senso misterioso delle sette stelle;
ché se sette erano magre, le altre sette erano ancor grassottelle.
Carlo Silva, 71 anni, abitava in Corso Lodi 108,
con la moglie e un figlio, impiegato alla "Dubied."
Aveva un secondo figlio sposato.
Aveva fatto il mediatore per tutta la vita
ma una lieve forma di paralisi lo aveva costretto
a muoversi con l'ausilio di un bastone.
Percepiva una esigua pensione, ma non aveva rinunciato
a recarsi ogni venerdì al settimanale convegno coi vecchi colleghi.
Bisogna andare da loro, stupidi come vipere, e dir loro:
Siamo fratelli: possediamo le ultime quattordici vacche:
la nostra azienda è in rovina,
lavoriamo con le nostre mani la terra
aiutati da un solo lavorante.
Non siamo più in grado di abitare in questo Paese
che se ne va per le strade nuove della storia
che hai veduto nella mia destra
e dei sette candelabri d'oro;
Gerolamo Papetti, 79 anni,
abitava alla cascina Ghisolfa di Rho
di cui era proprietario.
Aveva perso la moglie alcuni anni addietro.
Lascia tre figli, uno dei quali, Giocondo,

Io aveva accompagnato a Milano
ed è rimasto ferito in seguito allo scoppio.
Le sette stelle sono i sette Angeli delle sette Chiese
e i sette candelabri sono le sette Chiese.
Beh, non ho intenzione di scrivere l'intero Apocalisse:
ormai basta solo progettarlo;
e così le idee, basta enunciarle: realizzarle è superfluo.
In piena epoca industriale,
coltiviamo dunque la terra con le nostre mani, e un solo lavorante
Andremo dunque presto a vendere le nostre ultime 14 vacche
ai Vicini nel 1970 avanti Cristo.
No, davvero non si può,
l'ecolalie neanche notarili
vomitate su noi dai nostri coetanei al Governo
sono intollerabili. Caro Moravia, caro Antonioni,
andiamo di là.
Poi venni a casa.
La porta che dava sul corridoio della camera di mia madre
era aperta: da ciò arguii la sua inquietudine.
Essa ha ottant'anni, l'età di Gerolamo Papetti:
e penso a ciò che deve ancora soffrire.
Da letterato che fa della letteratura
dichiaro la mia solidarietà a "Potere Operaio"
e a tutti gli altri groupuscules di estrema sinistra,
Saragat non doveva fare un fascio di quell'erba:
e dunque sugli scudi Tolin.
Le sette Chiese sono su di noi, le zozze.
Scende la notte dello choc: il Naviglio va sottoterra
Tu ti suiciderai
se avevi tutto da guadagnare e nulla da perdere [3]
e quindi non sei un fascista di sinistra, che, poverino,
coi suoi ideali estremistici ora così tragicamente frustrati,
è divenuto mio caro fratello, e vorrei abbracciarlo forte;
tu ti ucciderai, fascista pazzo,
e il tuo suicidio non servirà ad altro

---

[3] Prevedendo in questi versi un suicidio, pensavo, con assurda ingenuità, che il colpevole che si sarebbe suicidato sarebbe stato un fascista.

che a dare una disgraziata traccia alla Polizia.
In attesa di essere vendute, queste nostre ultime 14 vacche
pascolano crepuscolari a Patmos
dove ci si limita a scrivere, dell'Apocalisse, il solo prologo.
Ma approfondiamo
(che altro non si fa a Patmos,
senza giungere mai a conclusioni diverse da quelle previste,
il deprimente disprezzo per la borghesia, ivi compresi
i morti di cui sopra, tutti onorabilmente vissuti infino alla fine)
proseguendo, proseguendo eroicamente,
dopo aver steso un velo sulla sconfitta dei giovani
A Efeso a Pergamo a Smirne a Tiatira a Sardi a Filadelfia e a Laodicea
vivono i lettori che disprezzano i buoni sentimenti
e sanno, sanno bene del binomio Autorità-Banalità,
ma ciò non esclude che anche tra loro
i buoni sentimenti siano poi del tutto screditati, anzi, anzi!
Ma le conclusioni di ogni approfondimento sono prevedibili, ripeto.
L'ultimo odor di stalla e di farina
e la stoffa che fuma nelle osterie con la latrina all'aperto
dove va gente che se la intende sull'onorabilità
e vi fa del razzismo romanico
unisce intellettuali di sinistra e fascisti a un unico culto
in via di estinzione: allontanando nel cosmo il punto di vista [4]
essi appaiono tutti raccolti a imprecare allo stesso tabernacolo;
la porta della storia è una Porta Stretta
infilarsi dentro costa una spaventosa fatica
c'è chi rinuncia e dà in giro il culo
e chi non ci rinuncia, ma male, e tiri fuori il cric dal portabagagli,
e chi vuole entrarci a tutti i costi, a gomitate ma con dignità;
ma son tutti là, davanti a quella Porta.

[4] Come nella Commedia pappo
coesiste notoriamente con pulcro.

Reprinted from Pier Paolo Pasolini, *Bestemmia* (Garzanti, 1993);
originally published in *Nuovi argomenti*, December, 1969.

PETER KAMMERER *Giuseppe, your thesis,*[1] *to summarize broadly, is that Pasolini's death was the work of an author, i.e. this particular death was planned by him in advance, announced in his writings, stage works, and films, then organized and finally carried out as a mythical, religious representation in a playing field in Ostia. It would thus be an integral part of Pasolini's idiom and a key to his entire oeuvre, which became fully meaningful only through this cultural rite*[2] *performed as a sacrifice.*

GIUSEPPE ZIGAINA You've said it. That's the framework in which, coordinated perfectly logically, Pasolini's "live novel" should be read as long as you accept the following premises:

1. Pasolini was not talking about death in general, but only about his own violent death, of which he was the author, not the victim.

2. As a "martyr director by choice," Pasolini wanted to bear witness to his "belief in the reality and efficacy of myth," the archetypal myth of Jonah, which he proclaimed in the film *The Gospel According to St. Matthew.*

3. Pasolini communicated his "death project" to the world as a "discourse in the language of jargon," i.e. in a cryptic language that has to be decoded.

KAMMERER *So that would mean that Pasolini decided on the place, time and manner of his death himself. The place was Ostia, the old* idroscalo *(seaplane dock) at the mouth of a branch of the Tiber. Nothing is left of the magic and mystery of this place today. Pasolini loved it, filmed scenes of* The Canterbury Tales *there, and*

In the
Firing Line

Pasolini's Signs of Life and Death
**Peter Kammerer in Conversation
with Giuseppe Zigaina**

The following is based on several conversations between Peter Kammerer— a longtime translator of Pasolini—and Giuseppe Zigaina, a friend of Pasolini's since the 1940s in Cervignano del Friuli. The conversations took place in January and February 2005.

precisely described his murder and the crime scene in 1964, in the poem Una disperata vitalità *(A Desperate Vitality). Ostia means not only river mouth, but also* hostia, *the sacrificial animal or the host of communion. Those are important clues for your theory about the location. But what about the timing?*

ZIGAINA A look at the perpetual calendar, which Pasolini consulted from the early 1960s on, reveals that in the critical period of his life Pasolini had only two dates when he could be killed according to the liturgical scheme he had planned. In order to underline the sacramental nature of his "cultural rite," he chose a day when All Souls (the Day of the Dead) fell on a Sunday (the Lord's Day). That was only the case in 1969 and 1975. Later possibilities such as 1980, 1986, 2003, and 2008 were exposed to the risk of unforeseen vicissitudes of life. Pasolini would then have been between fifty-eight and eighty-six, a long way from the age of the crucified Christ.

KAMMERER *How did you start your research into all this?*

ZIGAINA I began to delve into Pasolini's cryptic language so I could understand the meaning of the messages he was sending me. On November 6, 1975, i.e. after his death, I found a copy of the film of *Salò (120 Days of Sodom)* outside the door of my house, in Cervignano. This was a message from Pasolini telling me he was dead, because for him death had the same function as the director's cut, editing a film.

Disregarding subconscious remarks in his youth, Pasolini began to reveal his "death project" towards the end of the fifties. The first important revelation occurs in the poem *La Reazione Stilistica*, published in 1960. I first used the word "plurilinguism," to include the language of death, in a lecture at Berkeley called "Total Contamination in Pasolini."

KAMMERER *The poem* Patmos, *which dates from December 1969, contains—in your view—a coded message postponing the date from 1969 to 1975. It was published in* Trasumanar e organizzar *(a 1971 volume of poetry), which was regarded as largely incomprehensible.*

ZIGAINA *Trasumanar* is a word invented by Dante to describe performing a "(deed) beyond any human possibility." A meta-deed of this kind could, for example, be planning the resurrection of a human being. Dante writes: *Trasumanar significa per verba no si poria* (the meaning cannot be described in words). *Organizzar*, without the final *e* ending, is one of the most frequently used transitive verbs in the dialects of northeastern Italy. The title *Trasumanar e organizzar* is one of the many formulae with which Pasolini proclaimed his sacrificial death. Wittgenstein would describe a formula of this kind as an "elementary proposition with a truth function." But *trasumanar* is a verbal noun that in the rational sense has to be dependent on *organizzar*, which is essentially a transitive verb. In answer to the question: What did Pasolini do in his life? One might say he "organized his meta-deed," a passionately desired ascetic

[1] Giuseppe Zigaina, *Pasolini und der Tod. Mythos, Alchemie und Semantik des glänzenden Nichts. Eine Studie* (Munich, 1989); Giuseppe Zigaina and Christa Steinle, eds., *Pier Paolo Pasolini oder Die Grenzüberschreitung/ Organizzar il trasumanar.* Exh. cat. Neue Galerie am Landesmuseum Joanneum, Graz, et al. (Venice, 1995); Giuseppe Zigaina, *Pasolini e il suo nuovo teatro* (Venice, 2003).

[2] See Pier Paolo Pasolini, "Manifesto per un nuovo teatro," in *Nuovi Argomenti,* January-March 1968.

experience. Only if you switch the verbs round does the title lose its "absurdity" to become (in the words of the author) a "constantly recurring challenge to the self."

Pasolini published his volume at the end of the most critical phase of his life as an artist, the years between 1968 and 1970. He had to provide an explanation as to why he had put off the opportunity to express himself completely through death. As mentioned earlier, the first opportunity was in 1969, the second only in 1975. The postponement was due to meeting Maria Callas, and is evidence of the great partiality he had for her. It was a highly risky decision, as much on a level of linguistic expression as on an existential and religious level, to carry out a triple transgression that noone had ever thought of before and which prompted Pasolini to define himself as an "lab rabbit, not a man any more," as it says at the end of the poem *La Realtà* in *Poesia in Forma di Rosa*.

Pasolini subdivided *Trasumanar e organizzar* into a first and second book, as he had to help the reader to understand first the difficult phrase prior to 1969 and then the five years that followed.

KAMMERER *In the early poems, Pasolini always calls spring, very often the month of April, as the time of death.*

ZIGAINA Pasolini did indeed always write that he would have himself killed in spring, i.e. during the time of death and resurrection at Easter. But when he read Mircea Eliade, he discovered that "[the] myth" was to be celebrated in a night between fall and winter, on an especially holy day such as All Souls, when it falls on a Sunday.

In his *La Nuova Gioventù* volume of poetry there is a poem from 1974 called *Il Giorno della Mia Morte* (The Day of My Death; in the original Friulian: *Il Dì da la Me Muart),* with the words of the gospel according to St. John as a motto: "Except the wheatcorn fall into the ground and die, it bideth alone: but if it die, it bringeth forth much fruit." Pasolini had translated the poem from Friulian into Italian, omitting the expression *di vierta* (in spring), saying: *quando cambiano colore le foglie … uno è vissuto* (when the leaves lose their color … *one has lived),* or freely translated: "Between fall and winter, when the leaves change their color, I shall be dead."

It was virtually ignored that Pasolini, who often played a game of "imagining the future" with Elsa Morante, must have told this close friend something of his "project and secret," because in February 1970 he felt he should make the following declaration to her: "Oh Basilissa, what force of faith / what faith in force / he gets up after tumbling, as if nothing had happened, / with a casual smile. / 1970 has arrived, the year in which / the force of faith should have transfigured me / —then the fall, and I acted as if nothing had happened / oops, as you were, and whoever said / that 1970 should have been the start of something?"

The word "transfigured," which is a close parallel of *trasumanar* (to be parahuman says everything).

KAMMERER *We're gradually getting on to the poem* Patmos, *which is in the second book of* Trasumanar e organizzar, *where the poems tell a story like a novel about what is to happen in 1969 and afterwards.*

ZIGAINA That's right. The second book begins with the chapter *Charta (sporca)* (Letter of Manumission [dirty]), and this is followed by *Poemi Zoppicanti* (Limping Poems), both which allude ironically to the psychic and physical condition of the poet after 1969. A *charta* was a medieval word for a document of Roman origin given by a master to a freed slave so he could prove his freed status. Here it designates Pasolini's "freedom to choose death," and implies that the execution of his "project and secret" had been postponed from November 2, 1969 to 1975, a date that according to the perpetual calendar was the last date "free" for him to have himself killed. The last lines of *Charta (sporca)* say: "There is no reason / to write THE END after these words." The words written in capitals for emphasis do not mean the end of the poem but the end of this earthly life. The *charta* refers explicitly to the freedom which Pasolini defines as follows in *Empirismo Eretico* (Heretical Empiricism): "After long deliberations I finally understood that this mysterious word ultimately means in its profoundest sense nothing but the freedom to choose death."

It should be noted that Pasolini first prophesied his intention of dying in 1969 in the following lines of *Poesie Mondane* on June 12, 1962: "And I, / arrived too late for death, too soon / for the true life, savor the nightmare / of light like a sparkling wine." Decoded,

this means: in 1962, Pasolini discovered that at forty he had lived seven years longer than the crucified Christ, and at the same time he is seven years too early for his "true life," life after death. If we deduct the thirty-three years of Christ's life from Pasolini's forty, we get the number seven. If we add this to the year 1962, we get 1969, the date of the anticipated sacrificial death. Pasolini, in 1969, filmed *Medea,* which he planned to be his last work. With this in mind, he had spent the whole of the previous year preparing for it, because he wanted to show the "two stages" of his murder in it. The hasty completion of the five tragedies and *Manifesto per un Nuovo Teatro* (Manifesto for a New Theater) and finally the staging of *Orgia,* which was undoubtedly intended as a first version of *Medea,* support the same thesis.

KAMMERER *So it was meeting Maria Callas that induced Pasolini to put off his planned death? The poems he dedicated to her are moving and the finest in* Trasumanar e organizzar. *Some biographers say she committed suicide, in a sense like Pasolini.*

ZIGAINA "Today I'm the slave of a bottle of tablets. I think the end of life will be a pleasure for me." Maria Callas wrote that a few days before her death. But however that may be, it is certain that Pasolini reflected himself and his own story in Euripides' *Medea* and used Callas for it as a magic idol, so that Ninetto Davoli, who left Pasolini and married a woman, shows through as Jason, who betrays Medea. In *Medea,* Pasolini took the game of reflections, with which he had experimented in his previous film and theatre works, to such extremes that at the last moment he changed the screenplay so as to be able to say to Ninetto (via the figure of Jason) what he thought of him.

KAMMERER *To go back to the "dirty letter of manumission"…*

ZIGAINA Pasolini was obsessed with the idea of having to give an explanation for his "change of course" in postponing his death to 1975. On the back of the volume of poetry, he recommended the reader "who doesn't have much time to lose" at least to read *Charta (sporca)*.

His "project and secret" was still valid as such. It was only the execution of it that had become uncertain in dramatic fashion and had to be rethought, which Pasolini called "restoration from the left," as the poem of this name *(Restaurazione di sinistra)* suggests. He had to go back to the pre-1969 situation to get back on course, now aiming for 1975. That is the critical communication he makes in *Patmos*, where he proclaims November 2, All Souls Day, as the day of his ritual death. To say that, he quotes the title of a volume of poetry by the Milan dialect poet Delio Tessa: "*Lè il Dì di Mort, Alegher* (It's the Day of the Dead, Rejoice).

KAMMERER *The poem* Patmos *was written in the night of December 13–14, 1969, under the shock of the terrible news of the bomb attack in Milan. On December 12, the first major terrorist attack since World War II, at the Banca dell'Agricoltura in the Piazza Fontana, claimed the* lives of seventeen victims—fourteen in the bombing itself, three more in the following days—and injured eighty-five. At the time, Italy was in the travails of the "hot fall" of major social upheavals, which were now overshadowed by terrorism. A witch hunt followed for "anarchists and leftwing terrorists" on the back of statesman-like claims by leading politicians, while state officials concealed the actual criminals. Anarchist Giuseppe Pinelli, whose innocence is now proven, "fell" out of the window of the police headquarters during a hearing, and the police spread the story that this "suicide" was tantamount to an admission of guilt.

There is the following commentary on Patmos in the collected poems: "The text uses a typical technique of the neo-avant-garde (for example Nanni Balestrini) and consists of three different 'threads' that are cut out like in a collage and stuck together. The first thread quotes Revelation, the second a newspaper list of the victims, and the third polemically includes the declarations of President Giuseppe Saragat and powerful Christian Democratic politicians."[3]

ZIGAINA What do you think of that commentary? Anyone knows that Pasolini was always heavily critical of the new avant-garde, except Edoardo Sanguinetti in certain respects. To imply that he made use of their techniques seems rather far-fetched. As a secret alchemist, Pasolini drew on anything that he needed. That's well-known. But that he borrowed from Nanni Balestrini and newspaper lists I find unacceptable.

---

[3] Walter Siti, ed. *Pier Paolo Pasolini. Tutte le opere. Tutte le poesie,* vol. 2 (Milan, 2001), p. 1538.

Pasolini as Giotto in
The Decameron, 1970

KAMMERER *I'm interested in the connection Pasolini creates between the massacre in Milan, the Book of Revelation, and his own death, which the commentator ignores. Pasolini's tone reminds me of Heiner Müller, who establishes a similar link in his poem* Mommens Block *between the vision of St. John, the degeneracy of the Empire and his own situation: "Only St John on Patmos in a drug-induced fug / The heretic the death leader the terrorist / Saw the New Beast arising."*

ZIGAINA In my view, Pasolini established the connection because he was in a dramatic situation at the time. He always had to speak of himself, and also used the occasion to make his "revelation of the last future" that had obsessed him for twenty years. The political and anthropological message that always seems to feature in the foreground of Pasolini's writings needs to be supplemented with a mythical and religious dimension. That is the only way *Patmos* can be decoded. Let's look at the core of the poem.

Pasolini recalls the "Fascist Saturdays," when the war dead were called out by name, whereupon a loud *Presente!* was heard. This ceremony was the evocation: "You are alive in our hearts, even if you are dead forever." On the slopes of the karst, above the plain of Friuli and the Gulf of Trieste, is the military cemetery of Redipuglia with the graves of 70,000 Italian dead from World War I. Over the grave recesses, the names of the dead are listed alphabetically, each name having a large *Presente!* in horrible bronze lettering. Pasolini evokes this memory for the dead in Milan, using brackets as special punctuation marks. Russian linguist Yuri Tynyanov called them the "finest verbal element." The brackets are not used by the poet to try out new discoveries but to confess with a certain diffidence his "faith in the reality and efficacy of the myth" of dead and the resurrection.

On the night of December 13–14, 1969, with November 2 already behind him and having to be forgotten, Pasolini had the age of the Sceptics in mind; their way of postponing a "judgment" about the things of the world or leaving the meaning of words describing the world "in suspense." He recalled Tynyanov as quoted by Barthes and constructed his message in a code that no one has so far decoded. The key is the *Presente!*, which he brackets only three times. Once in giving the name of *Pietro* Dendena, another time with *Paolo* Gerli, and finally when Pietro and Paolo are united on the "Day of the Dead" (all present). That means that *Pietro Paolo Pasolini* will be "present" (i.e. dead) on November 2, 1975, the Day of the Dead. But the person writing this "revelation" is still alive. His *Presente!* is therefore in brackets.

The invention of Pasolini—the use he makes of the "newspaper list" of victims, which he compiles in no alphabetical or other order—consists in a coherent "secret language," a kind of argot, which the editors of the collected edition left hanging in a void. The trick with the brackets has a function in the discourse, the purpose of which is a verbal experiment is to highlight the names Pietro and Paolo among the names of the victims and link them with Pasolini's baptismal names.

Diego Velàzquez, *Apollo in Vulcan's Forge*, 1630 (detail)
Oil on canvas,
223 x 290 cm
Museo del Prado, Madrid

In a second operation, he prophesies—again with the help of brackets—the day of his death by quoting Delio Tessa, "it's the Day of the Dead (all present)." The brackets have a postponing or limiting function, because "all," meaning "both," i.e. Piero and Paolo Pasolini in fact, are not dead yet. With his use of cryptic language the author was provoking the critics, and in his "desperate vitality" takes advantage of them in a sarcastic, breezy way. He continues to speak in riddles when he says of Pietro Dendena: "I should not be surprised as a schizoid writer / if he appeared, just as he is, in a Prado oil painting / not even if he had a penchant for Inter." I translate this passage as follows: "I as a schizoid writer, split in two like my name Piero Paolo, would not be surprised to find myself exactly as I am in a Prado picture, with a penchant for Inter Milan since Bologna loses and brings me bad luck." In a visit to Madrid Pasolini had found himself in an oil painting in the Prado, a large painting Velàzquez painted in Rome in 1630, *Apollo in Vulcan's Forge.* The painter had used young people from the slums of Rome as models. Apollo, the god of prophecy and poetry, crowned with laurel and a halo of light, visits the forge. The similarity between Vulcan and Pasolini is stunning, and must have shaken the poet, not least because Vulcan shrinks back, his face full of fear, at the appearance of Apollo. The impression it made on him gave rise to the idea of dressing like Velàzquez's Vulcan to play a pupil of Giotto's in the film of *The Decameron.* Pasolini wears the same white band round his head and the leather apron.

KAMMERER *Seeing the way you interpret it and the critical importance you attribute to minimal clues, I realize the mistake I made in translating* Una Disperata Vitalità.[4] *Pasolini works with words like" "a demolition expert who unscrews the fuse of an unexploded bomb / and for a moment can remain in the world (in the sunlight amidst its modern apartment blocks) / or be extinguished for ever." At the time, the importance of minimal "displacements," on which life depends "from eternity to eternity," as it says in this poem published in 1964, was not clear.*

ZIGAINA Pasolini is of course the demolition expert handling mines. Ever more prey to his "uncontrolled, familiar death flushes," he worked continually on the attempt to organize the "displacement" of his earthly life to the life hereafter. Initially before 1969, then, after the "change of course," heading for 1975. His linguistic games are based—and no one has noticed this before— on the concept of displacement or shifts of meaning, which Freud uses in his work *Jokes and their Relationship with the Unconscious.* "The only true future life" for Pasolini depended on the "displacements/shifts of meaning" working and the viewer/reader understanding them correctly.

When Pasolini writes in *Empirismo Eretico:* "Kennedy expressed himself dying through his last action," the reader has to substitute the name of Pasolini for Kennedy. Only in this way does the message have a point, i.e. Pasolini expressed himself only in dying, through his last action. He is an author who knows

---

[4] Together with other key texts in Pier Paolo Pasolini, "Who is Me," in *Bestemmia: Tutte le poesie* (Milan, 1993).

what he wants, otherwise he would not have described himself as a "martyr director by choice." As a director and author, Pasolini use a lot of lists to point out to his audience/readers that his self-sacrifice constituted a monstrous "stylistic system" that would finally give the totality of the work a meaning. He summed it up clearly and deliberately in a sentence he wrote in 1964: "As long as I am not dead, no one can say they really know me."

KAMMERER *So Pasolini has a message he wants to communicate. But he says it and doesn't say it— he remains ambiguous because the message is monstrous and no reader at the time would have believed it. The key sentences of his announcements are linked with each other by a textual weave, by what Barthes calls the catalyses of narrative. Here we find political considerations, but also words without meaning—pure sound play. Poetry is always an interplay of sounds, associations, and analogies that determine the choice of words. You say the reader should not pay too much attention to this weave, otherwise the actual message will escape him.*

ZIGAINA I see you're quoting the introduction Barthes wrote in 1969 for the book *L'Analisi Strutturale de Racconto,* edited by Umberto Eco. Pasolini was so impressed by Eco's brilliant essay "The Narrative Structures in Fleming's Work"[5] that he sent him the coded message "I am neither Christ nor Fleming," saying in effect "it's always an honor to be the object of your investigations, but bear in mind I'm only half Fleming, the other half

Christ." This is said in the poem *Endoxa* dated April 28, 1969.[6]

KAMMERER *When he was investigating dreams, Freud discovered that repressed desires intensify and rearrange our dreams to escape inner censorship. Marginal things come to the fore, while desires of great sensory intensity are displaced to the periphery. Later he discovered that the same mechanisms operate with jokes.*

If we assume that Pasolini consciously used these techniques of the subconscious, that would mean for Patmos *that the massacre at the Piazza Fontana and the list of victims are at the center of the poem and are interpreted in the light of early Christianity (in analogy to the neo-Marxist sects of post-1968) but the essential meaning is scattered and displaced to the periphery. The first key statement in* Patmos *is in the line: "Only a suicide would put us on the trail of the one responsible for these tears." Pasolini adds a footnote to draw our attention: Take care, a suicide will be the key to the whole story. He begins to weave his own "death project" into the events, and continues: "Should their families weep; I speak of it as a writer." Pasolini always saw himself as a Mannerist. Emotion and traditional sympathy did not interest him, but the artistic truth of death certainly did.*

ZIGAINA Immediately after that, with a glance towards Freud, he continues: "Canons and tropes are available and replace emotion; / and it suffices to decide if the necessary mood is there / with all its features / (to barricade oneself behind vocabulary, this one, ruleless,

---

[5] Oreste Del Buono, ed, *Der Fall James Bond. 007 – Ein Phänomen unserer Zeit* (Munich, 1966).

[6] Printed in Pier Paolo Pasolini, *Medea. Un film di Pier Paolo Pasolini* (Milan, 1970).

unusual)." Canon means, in Greek, a stick, straight rod, or rule, and in the second figurative meaning "standard or rule." The lines can be read as follows: "The stick (to kill me with) and the phrases with their figurative meanings are ready, I need only decide, even if I have to use a vocabulary beyond any standard to express myself. The necessary mood is also there."

In his *Manifesto per un Nuovo Teatro* Pasolini uses the term *canone sospeso* or "suspended canon," which Barthes also uses, which could be literally translated (suspended rod) as well as figuratively to refer to his intention to have himself clubbed to death. The rod is a fundamental feature of the liturgy and the rite and goes back to the discovery of plowing. In the story of Cain and Abel, Cain kills his shepherd brother Abel with a stick. Later the stick was, and still is in many places, a basic instrument for threshing corn.

KAMMERER *Pasolini invokes all fourteen dead in the Milan bomb attack by name. All of them were livestock dealers or farmers blown apart by a bomb, victims of the industrial world erupting into their world. Pasolini depicts the agricultural milieu of the victims, using the town of Lodi as a code and describing its avenues, smells, materials, and humidity. The corpses were "reduced to stumps," and Pasolini adds contemptuously: "Letting yourself be found in such condition is a poor show of good manners / by those men of honor."*

ZIGAINA Pasolini's discourse is full of sarcastic allusions in which stylistic elements stand out that are perfectly coordinated logically. "Letting yourself be found in such condition is a poor show of good manners" and is "unacceptable for a serious man who is concerned with agriculture! / just as if we were still in 1944." And "In the middle of an industrial age / we till the soil with our hands and a single laborer." Undoubtedly Pasolini is referring to himself here. He is the one who is concerned with agriculture, peasants, and archaic fertility rites and now identifies himself with the victims. It is his fate, like the Naviglio canal in Milan mentioned later, to go underground in his career. Pasolini already used this image earlier: "There are rivers called Reca and here the two Timavos." The Reca and Timavo rivers make up a single river called the Reca on the Slovenia side but becomes the Timavo when it vanishes among the rocks of the karst, only to surface again shortly before emptying into the Gulf of Trieste. Pasolini wrote the poem *Reca* for me in 1969, referring to the two of us using the image of two rivers. He used the Slovene word *Reca* in the plural and annotated it with three dots.

KAMMERER *"The Naviglio goes under the ground / you will kill yourself / if you have everything to gain and nothing to lose." This announcement, related to Pasolini, makes sense if linked with the conclusion of* Patmos. *What Pasolini wants is to gamble on a single turn of the cards in order to enter real history. But: "The gate of history is a narrow gate / to filter in requires enormous effort." Earlier Pasolini had already said: "We are no longer in a position to live in this country / which passes on to new roads of history" (which he wants nothing to do with). And* *again: "We shall soon sell our last fourteen cows / to the neighbors in 1970 before Christ." What does that mean?*

ZIGAINA The story of the fourteen cows in *Patmos* can be linked through the dark channels of the unconscious with Pasolini's vision from seven years earlier. On June 12, 1962 he realized he was forty years old and therefore had already lived seven years longer than Christ. The number seven must have had a magical resonance when he thought about death. In my view, Pasolini was already consulting the perpetual calendar even then, because as a "Christian of the early Church " he believed in the Kabbala, i.e. magic, and in the quest for a death day between fall and winter when All Souls falls on a Sunday, he found the year 1969. For Pasolini, the "red April of youth had passed."

The lines you mention could be decoded as follows: "I don't feel able to live any longer in a world that without knowing it doesn't want me any more. But I, a force of the past and more modern than any modernist, will conclude the last fourteen years of my earthly life in 1970 before Christ." That's Pasolini in *Patmos*. In 1962 he had written, and I'll quote it again, "And I, / arrived too late for death, too soon / for the true life, savor the nightmare / of light like a sparkling wine." Seven years too late to die like Christ at thirty-three, and seven years too early if 1969 was to be the year of death. The fourteen cows Pasolini mentions in *Patmos* recall the dream of the Pharaoh, which Joseph interpreted as seven years of abundance and seven years of drought. Pasolini aligns himself with Joseph and the Pharaoh to tell the world he will sell his last fourteen cows to the neighbors, i.e. the fourteen victims of the massacre of Milan (in the neighboring graves). Why he writes "1970 before Christ" will become clear shortly. We can definitely state that Pasolini was planning for the "spring of [his] resurrection" in 1962 he constantly refers to in his poems, that he then postponed the day to the fall, and that he fixed the time, date, and organization of his self-sacrifice as a proper ritual in advance. He wanted to not only underline its sacramental nature thereby, but also the fact that no one had ever made such a decision before. Ever since he had announced this in 1962, Pasolini lived in the nightmare of his seven-year arrears vis-à-vis Christ, his archetypal hero. He names the actual date of his death, November 2, for the first time in *Patmos*, in the chapter of *Poemi zoppicanti,* and only after the deadline had expired. Writing "1970 before Christ" was to draw the reader's attention to the Kabbalist play with the number fourteen. It corresponds to the number of dead in Milan, the sum of seven years' arrears and seven years advance and also the sum of the digits in 1940 and 1490 in the lines: "No serenade was sung in that year of 1940; / since 1490 people had worked honestly on their knitted socks." The disconcerting "before Christ" is a kind of "displacement," and is based on the hypothesis that the death of Christ is still to come, because Pasolini saw himself as a mirror image of the living Christ, with whom he identified himself. Shortly before he wrote *Patmos,* he sent Umberto Eco the message in the poem *Endoxa* that we have already quoted: "I am neither Christ nor Fleming."

KAMMERER *The detail "before Christ" looks like a mistake. And the switched years 1940 and 1490. It's very contrived word play.*

ZIGAINA Pasolini always considered Freud to be a great writer. He studied the techniques that Freud discovered in *Jokes and their Relationship with the Unconscious,* which make jokes so important for human relationships. The techniques that Freud called "humor with verbal displacement" lend Pasolini's language an absolutely transgressive character. A joke Freud investigated based on the double meaning of the word *leben* [life] fascinated Pasolini particularly.

A Jewish marriage broker assures the suitor that the girl's father is no longer alive [*im Leben*]. After the betrothal it turns out that the father is still *im Leben* and serving out a prison sentence. The suitor reproaches the broker. "Now," says the latter, "Don't worry. It's not a life [*ein Leben*]?" Pasolini uses puns of this kind in several places in *Empirismo Eretico,* also as a challenge to the intelligence of his readers. In *Il Cinema Impopolare* (Unpopular Cinema), he concludes some complex linguistic word play with this provocative sentence: "But the essential thing (for the author) is to stay alive," without saying whether he was referring to physical life or the afterlife (i.e. fame).

On the same page, nine lines on, Pasolini says of underground cinema that "martyr directors are stylistically always in the firing line, by choice—i.e. in the front line of linguistic transgressions. Through constantly breaching the code (i.e. needling the world that uses it) and continually provoking criticism, they finally get what they aggressively seek out—to be injured and killed with the weapons they themselves offer the enemy."

Here again Pasolini does not explain to the reader or audience that he would betake himself to the "frontline of linguistic transgressions," i.e. to the football ground in Ostia in order to stage the most monstrous and incomprehensible transgression—his own violent death as language, which would first give his entire oeuvre its logic. That tallied with his theory that "only the death of the hero is a play; only that is beneficial."

KAMMERER *What role does the unconscious play in Pasolini, if he works so consciously with the techniques of dreams or puns?*

ZIGAINA We should not mix things up. Pasolini constructs his puns quite cold-bloodedly. He does not work with his own dreams or those of others. He is just as uninterested in the connection between puns and the unconscious. His unconscious was undoubtedly in the darkness of some hellish region. In *La Reazione Stilistica* of the late 1950s, he had referred pedagogically to the fact that his language "is supplemented, let no one forget, by what will be and is not yet," whereby he obviously means his violent death as non-verbal language. If he turns towards death without mentioning it and says: "You are singling me out and giving me the certainty of life," he is referring to his continued existence in the memory of mankind. He was therefore anticipating the prophecy about himself he made in 1974: "Born to be one, I shall be double … one, but double." He is like an alchemist; he works secretly on two different but parallel levels: *tam ethice quam phisice,* on a spiritual as much as on a physical level.

Pasolini discovered his alchemistic side by reading Jung. This is how he came to work with the double meaning of the word *petrolio,* defining it as a form of life whose rules must be written *in corpore vili*—in a vile body—i.e. in the form of his massacred body. The word *petrolio* includes Pasolini in his totality as a man and author. It is a seal with two sides—on one side it features as *oleum petrae* (the black fluid that occasionally gushes from certain rock configurations), on the other side it is *olio di Pietro,* the abstract, the essence, the substance of Pietro (Paolo Pasolini). This substance becomes an ambiguous emblem of our time, whose expression is sophisticated means of communication and preventive wars, in which these are skillfully used.

KAMMERER *The posthumously published novel* Petrolio *is about modern disasters, oil, and terrorism.* Patmos *was already apocalyptic. Is there a connection between the spreading violence and Pasolini's obsessive death wish or its execution?*

ZIGAINA There was certainly at least an indirect connection between the massacre in Milan and Pasolini's suicide. These are phenomena of social and political self-destruction that we have experienced for years. The violent death of Pasolini was anticipated by him in numerous messages and could be taken as a stylistic sign of the present day a decade before it happened, a "symptom whose meaning is revealed only to experts," as Pasolini put it.

KAMMERER *I was particularly impressed by a passage from Pasolini's last interview. There he says: "The desire to kill prevails here. And this desire links us like unfortunate brothers of an unfortunate failure of a whole social system." That throws light on an important part of* Patmos *that is difficult to understand, where after the announcement of the suicide it reads: "And so you are not a left-wing fascist who, poor man, / with his now so tragically frustrated extremist ideals, / has become my dear brother and whom I should like to hug; / you will kill yourself, crazy fascist." Neither Pinelli nor Pasolini are fascists, but united in being "unfortunate," if we "shift the viewpoint into the cosmos."*

You spoke just now of a particular expertise that Pasolini expects of the reader. But he does not divulge his sources. He very often quotes Freud, but Jung and Wittgenstein almost never.

ZIGAINA Wittgenstein—the linguistic philosopher who influenced Pasolini enormously—was quoted twice by him in the message to the conference of the Partito Radicale, a few hours before Pasolini had himself murdered. The punning technique he had learned from Freud and the sarcastic ends he used it for is additionally complicated by the alchemistic procedures he had learned from Jung. That has definitely to be taken into account. An example: in a poem of March 1969, Pasolini informed the world that his violent death was a "commissioned work" by him. That too is a formula that Wittgenstein described as an "elementary proposition with a truth function." Why an elementary proposition? Because the formula, as in *Organizzar il trasumanar,* is reduced to two essential concepts that say "everything" that happened in the early hours of November 2, 1975. The "extreme action" in the sacred district of Ostia was in its "truth function" the repetition of the myth of death and resurrection, i.e. a prayer that Pasolini himself ordered, i.e. "commissioned." "Order" and "organize" are absolutely unambiguous verbal forms and accordingly can only be interpreted in one way. In the poem *Preghiera su commissione* (Prayer to Order) it says: I have a poetic notion of the grass. / And I know poetry's excess. / Which is why I have commissioned lines, / for my consecration (!) / … to pray in this sacred space / (where, to tell the truth, I don't walk with bare feet."

Versi means death in Pasolini. He writes: "I pass on, in a line of verse," which means "by dying, I make poetry." But the stylistic sign that I call alchemy, one of the special minimalist signs that characterize the language of Pasolini is the exclamation mark in brackets that leaves his "consecration" in suspense. Because Pasolini was still alive when he wrote these lines. That he would not enter the "sacred space" with bare feet is to be expected, because as a "Christian of the early Church," unlike in Islam, he was not expected to take off his shoes. We find the whole process confirmed again in *Bestia da stile:* "The yellowing grass that survives every season, / and the smooth stones, that is my theater … Just because it's a holiday. / I wish to die of humiliations out of protest. / I want them to find me with bared genitals, / and with trousers stained with white semen."

KAMMERER *So we have here the same use of stylistic signs as in* Patmos. *Another last question about Michelangelo Antonioni and Alberto Moravia: one of them, wrote Pasolini, "laughs with his eyes," the other is absent-minded. In the evening of December 12, when the news of the terrorist attack was broadcast on television, Pasolini and Antonioni were at Moravia's house.*

ZIGAINA I don't think Pasolini and Moravia ever really understood each other. Partly because, unlike his other friend Elsa Morante, he never told him of his "project and secret." He often said to him with tenderness and affection: "You see, Alberto, what counts is the mercy of insight into things," Moravia never understood what he was talking about. Antonioni was in certain respects more receptive to this side of Pasolini. In *Patmos,* it says: "And anyone in shock laughs with the eyes of Antonioni / who confirms as the Word of God and witness of Jesus Christ / and also Pasolini laughs at / everything that he has seen, / whereas Moravia is absent-minded, blessed those that read there, / and blessed those that here there the words of this prophecy." The contamination of the depiction of the situation with the apocalypse is clear. We have already talked about that.

KAMMERER *All the sides of Pasolini we are long familiar with: his narcissistic dilation in the autobiography, his life as a "live novel," his archaic, modernist mysticism, his concept of works of art as actions, his tendency towards performance—what you have told me puts it all in a new light. Even the much-quoted words from* Who is Me: *"I should like to express myself through examples. / Throw my body into the struggle." And: "Actions of life are only communicated, / and they are themselves poetry, / because, I repeat, there is no poetry except real action."*

ZIGAINA That says it all. Death, Pasolini's "extremest action," is poetry. He first communicated this action symbolically in Section 3 of *Una Disperata Vitalità,* then he staged it on the football pitch in Ostia, thereby reaffirming his faith in the reality and power of myth, particularly the myth of Jonah, whom he discovered and proclaimed through the figure of Christ in the film *The Gospel According to St. Matthew.* The *Preghiera su Commissione,* the "prayer to order," celebrated in that "sacred space" in the Tiber estuary in Ostia, is an example of a mythical event. It is the "topic" of which Pasolini says in *Una Disperata Vitalità:* "That's why I can write about topics and laments / and also prophecies." And once again we come up against a pun which the critics have done nothing to decode these thirty years. Because *treni,* trains, which lament with whistles in the distance in Section 5, become *treni,* threnodies, lamenting the dead, in the last part.

Peter Kammerer *teaches sociology at the University of Urbino. He has published works on Heiner Müller, Pier Paolo Pasolini, Jean-Marie Straub, Antonio Gramsci, and St. Francis of Assisi.*

Giuseppe Zigaina *is a painter, draftsman, graphic designer, and writer. He became a friend of Pier Paolo Pasolini in 1946.*

P.P.P.

PIER PAOLO PASOLINI

Proletariat
Paradise
Province

The Changing of Culture by the "New Fascism"

Loris Lepri   The death of experience is due not least to things taking on a shape under the law of their purely functional nature that limits handling them to mere functional purposes, without tolerating an excess, whether of freedom of behavior or the independence of things that survive as a core of experience because they were not consumed by the moment of action.

Theodor Adorno: "Aphorism 19: Do Not Knock," *Minima Moralia*

On February 1, 1975, an article by Pier Paolo Pasolini appeared in the daily newspaper, *Corriere della Sera*. It was titled "Il vuoto di potere in Italia" (The Power Vacuum in Italy). Using the metaphor of the "disappearance of the glowworm," Pasolini describes the decade between 1960 and 1970 as a moment of transition between two epochs in the history of humanity. The new, forthcoming era is the "rule of consumerism and mass hedonism—a development that, especially in Italy, has triggered an anthropological revolution."

According to the logic of the neo-capitalist revolution, the consumer-oriented society (to paraphrase Pasolini) is notable not only for overproduction—in contrast to the production of essential goods—but also for a "new humanity," a new form of social relationships. The consequence of the diktat of the hedonistic ideology was a profound anthropological change in man. The new "culture" wants people who have lost every tie with their own past and their own values (thrift, morality), people who live in an imponderable state wherein consumption and hedonistic satisfaction count as the only values worth striving for.

Little more than a year earlier, Pasolini had identified the persuasive power of television as a key agent in implementing this new social model in the Italy. In "Sfida ai dirigenti della televisione" (A Challenge to Those who Run Television), printed in *Corriere della Sera* on December 9, 1973, he outlined how the ideological barrage of television was expressed in "things" by means of a bodily mimetic language, a language of behavior. The male and female models singled out for emulation were not so much described as dramatized (young men on motorcycles, girls advertising toothpaste, et al). The heroes of television propaganda churned out millions of similar ordinary heroes.

The effectiveness of this propaganda lay in its perfect pragmatism, the capacity to dictate a uniform cultural model that was on the point of destroying, or had already destroyed, all the specific local forms of culture that life had evolved. The cultural adaptation to this "center of consumerism" led to the decline of the peasant universe to which the urban sub-proletariat and the working classes belonged.

The notion of a "consumerist center," ultimately a place of an alienated cultural, political, and economic centralization, clearly has its roots in Marxism. It cannot help but remind us of the famous passage in the *Communist Manifesto*:

"The bourgeoisie have subjected the land to the dominance of the cities. They have created enormous cities. They have greatly increased the number of the urban population relative to the rural population and thereby snatched a large proportion of the population away from the lunacy of living on the land. Just as they have made the land dependent on the city, so they have made the barbarian and half-barbarian countries dependent on the civilized countries, the peasant nations on the bourgeois nations, east on west."

Pasolini was presumably alluding to this passage when, without directly quoting it, he spoke of the "genocide by the bourgeoisie of certain layers of the suppressed classes" during a discussion at *Unità*'s Milan

Risposta su Moravia. Le mie proposte su scuola e Tv (Response to Moravia: My Proposals for School and TV), by Pier Paolo Pasolini in *Corriere della sera*, October 29, 1975

festival in the summer of 1974. This genocide, Pasolini thought, had been carried out on the "people" (in Antonio Gramsci's sense) of contemporary Italy, by means of the population's general adaptation to the lifestyles of the bourgeoisie.

According to Pasolini, the antecedent for the adaptation, flattening out, and destruction of archaic cultural pluralism caused by the neo-capitalist, industrial leveling out was Hitler's Germany, where the "values of the various particular cultures were destroyed during the violent *gleichschaltung* (forcing into line) accompanying industrialization. The subsequent liberation of great masses of people who no longer belonged to the old (peasant, laboring) culture but were also not

Pasolini with Carlo di Carlo
and others at a protest march
against the International Film
Festival in Venice, late 1968

yet modern (bourgeois) constituted the potential of the barbaric, mentally deranged, unpredictable Nazi shock troops ("Il vuoto di potere in Italia," 1975). The year before he had already lamented (during the 1974 *Unità* discussion):

"When I see young people giving up the old traditional values and absorbing the new models capitalism prescribes them, and in doing so accepting a certain kind of inhumanity and wretched aphasia and the brutal loss of their own critical faculties, behaving both passively and inflammatorily at the same time, it reminds me of the SS, who were just like that."

The new cultural model offered to Italians was unique. Conformism manifested itself first of all in experience, existentially, and therewith in the body, in behavior, where values are lived out prior to being articulated in the new bourgeois consumer culture. These were replaced by the values of "the new and most repressive totalitarianism ever seen," according to his "Lettera aperta a Italo Calvino. Pasolini: quello che rimpiango" (Open Letter to Italo Calvino. Pasolini: What I Mourn For), printed in *Paese Sera* on July 8, 1974.

The new generation's cultural toeing of the line left visible evidence in physical and behavioral characteristics. To this day, the most impressive and disquieting description of this phenomenon was formulated by Pasolini in an article for *Corriere della Sera* on June 24, 1974, under the title "Il potera senza volto" (The Faceless Power): "In a group of young people, you can no longer distinguish a worker physically from a student, or a fascist from an anti-fascist—which was still possible

During the Circeo hearing, in the courtroom in Latina, 1962

in 1968." In these real-life conditions, the "new power" had formed in the shape of total fascism. According to Pasolini, whereas the fascism of the 1920s was not yet in a position to damage the physical and existential identity of the Italian people, the "new fascism" had wrought an anthropological mutation in Italians with the weapons of manipulating consciousness and habits (where the influence of television was fundamental), instilling new patterns of feeling, new ways of thinking and behaving, and new cultural models—the models of the "new power," the "society of consumerism."

That is the picture of Italian society that Pasolini drew in the the last years of his life, 1973 to 1975, and it is not difficult to understand why many people are inclined to attribute a certain prophetic dimension to his views.

Loris Lepri *is a film historian and curator at the Centro Studi – Archivio Pier Paolo Pasolini in Bologna.*

The Last Interview

Philippe Bouvard in Conversation
with Pier Paolo Pasolini

This is a translated transcript of Pier Paolo Pasolini's last television interview on October 31, 1975. During the interview Bouvard posed the questions in French, while Pasolini responded in Italian.

PHILIPPE BOUVARD *Pier Paolo Pasolini, you were a pioneer of cinematic art. Has the rise of erotic cinema and pornographic movies rendered you obsolete?*

PIER PAOLO PASOLINI Yes, I certainly feel obsolete, and given the way things are right now, I'm even inclined to drop my *Triology of Life* from *Il Decameron* to *Il fiore delle Mille e una notte* altogether.

BOUVARD *Have filmmakers gone too far, do you think?*

PASOLINI No—at least not filmmakers; the producers of porn films, perhaps.

BOUVARD *Will your latest movie provoke yet another scandal when it's released? [The reference is to* Salò o le 120 giornate di Sodoma *which was not released until after Pasolini's death.]*

PASOLINI To scandalize is a right just as to be scandalized is a pleasure in my view. A person who deliberately forgoes this pleasure is a moralist, or rather a so-called moralist.

BOUVARD *Is sex political?*

PASOLINI Of course.

BOUVARD *And scatological language?*

PASOLINI That too—nothing is really apolitical.

BOUVARD *And cannibalism?*

PASOLINI In some circles, it's a political reality, in others a political metaphor.

BOUVARD *Is cannibalism the best way of getting rid of one's political adversaries, do you think?*

PASOLINI Well you know I recently made two modest proposals along the lines of Jonathan Swift—that all the teachers in our state schools and all the directors of Italian television should be devoured.

BOUVARD *But wouldn't they be rather hard to digest?*

PASOLINI Oh, I think our stomachs would be strong enough to handle it …

BOUVARD *Are you still nursing the same old hatred of all things bourgeois and of the bourgeoisie?*

PASOLINI It's not hatred—sometimes it's rather more than that and sometimes rather less. These days, though, I'm afraid I have to manage without this kind of hatred, because everyone in Italy is now bourgeois.

BOUVARD *And if it is to the bourgeoisie that you owe the success of one of your films, does that make you sad?*

PASOLINI The success or otherwise of a film is never dictated by the bourgeoisie, but rather by the educated elite, to whom I myself belong, and by the movie-going masses, which include both the bourgeois and the poor sub-proletariat.

BOUVARD *Why are you no longer politically active?*

PASOLINI What do you mean?

BOUVARD *You're no longer a political activist.*

PASOLINI Oh, yes I am—and more than ever before, in fact. True, I never belonged to a political party. I'm an independent leftist and a Marxist, and more politically active now than I've ever been before.

BOUVARD *Do you ever find yourself longing for the days when passers-by would hurl abuse at you on the street?*

PASOLINI But they still do …

BOUVARD *And do you derive some kind of pleasure from that?*

PASOLINI I certainly don't reject it—I'm not a moralist after all.

BOUVARD *Which professional title do you yourself prefer: poet, novelist, writer of dialogue, scriptwriter, actor, critic, or director?*

PASOLINI In my passport I call myself simply "writer."

Casting *The 120 Days of Sodom*, 1975

BOUVARD *Why was the shooting of* Salò o le 120 giornate di Sodoma *so shrouded in secrecy?*

PASOLINI It was shot in secret because every work is created in secret. Having said that, I tried to protect this work even more than most, because the dangers threatening it were so immediate and imminent—not that I took any special precautions.

BOUVARD *What kind of "immediate dangers" are you talking about?*

PASOLINI The appearance of some moralist who would reject the pleasure of being scandalized.

BOUVARD *The movie is set in a puppet republic somewhere in Italy during World War II—a republic that is perhaps reminiscent of Vichy France during the Nazi occupation?*

PASOLINI Of course, it's the exact equivalent of Vichy France.

BOUVARD *And where was this republic?*

PASOLINI In northern Italy. And its capital was Salò—hence the title: *Salò.*

BOUVARD *And who set it up?*

PASOLINI Hmm, I think it was Mussolini himself, who was forced to do it by the Nazis.

BOUVARD *Do you regard this as a period of great degeneracy?*

PASOLINI Well the Hitler regime was certainly degenerate, but not Western capitalism in general.

BOUVARD *We know that in this movie, a hundred or so young men and women have to endure all kinds of cruelty and violence—that they are tortured and humiliated in the worst ways imaginable. How on earth did you recruit all these young people?*

PASOLINI Well to be honest, I followed de Sade, for whom the number four was a magic number. And there are about twenty victims in all, not a hundred. I recruited them the same way I always do, by screening thousands of people and then selecting the ones who seemed most suitable.

BOUVARD *So are they masochists?*

PASOLINI If I selected them, then yes, they are.

P.P.P.

PIER PAOLO PASOLINI

Primo
Piano
Personale

Filmography

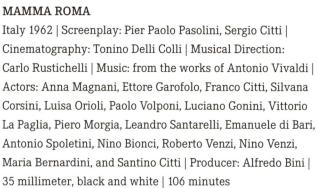

ACCATTONE

Italy 1961 | Screenplay: Pier Paolo Pasolini, with Sergio Citti |
Cinematography: Tonino Delli Colli | Musical Direction: Carlo
Rustichelli | Music: from the works of Johann Sebastian Bach |
Actors: Franco Citti, Franca Pasut, Paola Guidi, Silvana
Corsini, Adriana Asti, et al. | Producer: Alfredo Bini |
35 millimeter, black and white | 120 minutes

Accattone, the principal character of Pasolini's first film, is
a young man from the outskirts of Rome. Like his friends,
he does whatever he has to to get by; the woman he lives
with, Maddalena, works for him as a prostitute. When she is
thrown in prison by the police, Accattone is forced to make a
living on his own. He falls in love with Stella, with whom he
dreams of having a bourgeois future and a family, but he ends
up prostituting her, as well. When Maddalena reports him to
the authorities as a pimp and a thief, events take a predictable
course. Accattone dies attempting to flee a life from which
there is no escape. His last words are, "Now things are going well." In objective, almost documentary black-and-white
images, the film evokes the hopelessness of life in the Italian
suburbs in the 1960s.

MAMMA ROMA

Italy 1962 | Screenplay: Pier Paolo Pasolini, Sergio Citti |
Cinematography: Tonino Delli Colli | Musical Direction:
Carlo Rustichelli | Music: from the works of Antonio Vivaldi |
Actors: Anna Magnani, Ettore Garofolo, Franco Citti, Silvana
Corsini, Luisa Orioli, Paolo Volponi, Luciano Gonini, Vittorio
La Paglia, Piero Morgia, Leandro Santarelli, Emanuele di Bari,
Antonio Spoletini, Nino Bionci, Roberto Venzi, Nino Venzi,
Maria Bernardini, and Santino Citti | Producer: Alfredo Bini |
35 millimeter, black and white | 106 minutes

To her customers she is an ordinary Roman prostitute; to her
friends, however, she is known as Mamma Roma. Dissatis-
fied with her existence, she longs to lead a settled and finan-
cially stable life. When her pimp gets married and leaves the
city, her vision moves within reach. Her sixteen-year-old son
Ettore has grown up in the country, and she decides to bring
him to live with her in Rome. However, she is determined
that he learn nothing of the life she has led, so Mamma Roma
moves with him into a lower middle-class residential neigh-
borhood and earns her money selling vegetables from a mar-
ket stand. She spoils Ettore, for whom she dreams of a better
life than her own. The young man, however, turns out to be
a committed loafer; he goes astray, is arrested, and dies. For
Mamma Roma it means the collapse of her whole world. The
film stars the Italian character actress Anna Magnani in one
of her greatest roles.

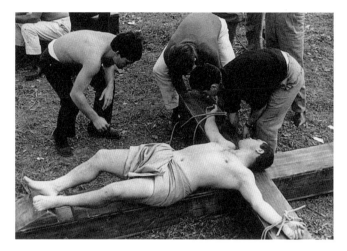

LA RICOTTA
(LET'S HAVE A BRAINWASH), EPISODE FROM ROGOPAG

Italy 1962 | Screenplay: Pier Paolo Pasolini | Cinematography: Tonino Delli Colli | Musical Direction: Carlo Rustichelli | Music: selections from the work of Alessandro Scarlatti, Giuseppe Verdi, et al. | Actors: Orson Welles, Mario Cipriani, Laura Betti, Edmonda Aldini, Ettore Garofalo, Vittorio La Paglia, Tomas Milian, Franca Pasut, et al. | Producer: Alfredo Bini | 35 millimeter, color and black and white | 40 minutes

A team is shooting a film about the passion of Christ. The director is a Marxist, intellectual filmmaker played by Orson Welles, who lounges in the director's chair making sarcastic comments about the world. Stracci, an extra who plays a thief, comes from extremely modest circumstances. With tricks and ruses, he manages to set aside rations for his starving family, but at a certain point his own hunger gets the upper hand, and he frantically gulps down enormous quantities of food—including the ricotta cheese of the title—and dies. Stracci's death on the cross is discovered as the producer, with an illustrious entourage, arrives at the location, where a richly set table is waiting. *La ricotta* was originally conceived as an independent feature film, but later, at the suggestion of the producer, became part of the episodic film *RoGoPaG,* with contributions by directors Roberto Rossellini, Jean-Luc Godard, Pasolini, and Ugo Gregoretti.

LA RABBIA
(RAGE)

Italy 1963 | Screenplay: Pier Paolo Pasolini | Commentary read by Giorgio Bassani (poetry) and Renato Guttuso (prose) | Music assembled by Pier Paolo Pasolini | Producer: Gastone Ferrante | 35 millimeter, black and white | 53 minutes

This film originally consisted of two different parts. Pasolini was responsible for the first, while the second was made by Giovanni Guareschi and withdrawn after protests over its racist nature. The subjects making up the montage, which was put together out of documentary material from newsreels of the 1950s and 1960s, are current events from various regions of the world, including the popular uprising in the DDR, the coronation of Elizabeth II, Bourgiba's entrance into independent Tunisia, the Hungarian popular uprising, Castro's victory in Cuba, the election of Pope John XXIII, appearances by the actresses Ava Gardner and Sophia Loren, the assassination of the Congolese independence fighter Patrice Lumumba, the end of the Algerian War, and the death of Marilyn Monroe. Pasolini added lyrical texts to the documentary images, creating, according to Alberto Moravia, an "original and personal, and therefore poetic, interpretation of the events of the last fifteen years."

COMIZI D'AMORE
(LOVE MEETINGS)

Italy 1963 | Screenplay: Pier Paolo Pasolini (commentary) | Cinematography: Mario Bernardo, Tonino Delli Colli | Participants: Pier Paolo Pasolini, Alberto Moravia, Cesare Musatti, Susanna Pasolini, Camilla Cederna, Oriana Fallaci, Giuseppe Ungaretti, Graziella Granata, the Bologna football team, et al. | Producer: Alfredo Bini | 35 millimeter, black and white | 92 minutes

Pasolini conducts interviews on the subject of sexuality. He asks hundreds of Italians in the country and big cities (passers-by, farmers, workers, football players, students, and tradespeople) of various ages and social classes their opinions on eroticism and love, homosexuality, divorce, and prostitution. Michel Foucault wrote of the film: "This is an invaluable document … After the long reign of what we are a bit too quick to call Christian morality, it might have been expected that, in the Italy of the early 1960s, the 'sexual' was ready to boil over. Not at all. Those who are questioned stubbornly insist on couching their answers in legalistic language … as if Italian society had not yet found a voice within this climate of public volubility in sexual matters that our media are propagating today. What runs through the film is … an uncertainty vis-à-vis a new regime, which was just emerging in Italy at the time, the regime of tolerance."

IL VANGELO SECONDO MATTEO
(THE GOSPEL ACCORDING TO ST. MATTHEW)

Italy 1964 | Screenplay: Pier Paolo Pasolini; adapted from the Gospel of Matthew | Cinematography: Tonino Delli Colli | Music: Johann Sebastian Bach, Wolfgang Amadeus Mozart, Sergei Prokofiev, Anton Webern, Luis Enrique Bacalov, et al. | Actors: Enrique Irazoqui, Margherita Caruso, Susanna Pasolini, Marcello Morante, Mario Socrate, Settimo Di Porto, Giorgio Agamben, Natalia Ginzburg, et al. | Producer: Alfredo Bini | 35 millimeter, black and white | 142 minutes

This film adaptation of the Gospel of Matthew on the birth, works, death, and resurrection of Jesus is scrupulously faithful to the letter and structure of the original. It is set by the director—an atheist and a Marxist—in the barren mountain landscape of southern Italy. Pasolini dispensed with professional actors altogether; his mother, Susanna, plays Mary as an old woman, and for the crowd scenes he drew from the local residents. The film derives an essential moment of tension from its use of music, which ranges from classical choral music to American spirituals. An homage to Pope John XXIII, the film was Pasolini's first international success despite vehement criticism from all political camps. He won the special jury prize at the Venice Film Festival, and the film met with widespread approval when it was shown at the Second Vatican Council. While searching for a location to shoot, Pasolini made the film *Sopraluoghi in Palestina per Il Vangelo secondo Matteo* (16 millimeter, black and white, 55 minutes).

UCCELLACCI E UCCELLINI
(HAWKS AND SPARROWS)

Italy 1965 | Screenplay: Pier Paolo Pasolini | Cinematography: Tonino Delli Colli, Mario Bernardo | Music: Ennio Morricone | Actors: Totò, Ninetto Davoli, Femi Benussi, Rossana Di Rocco, Lena Lin Solaro, Riccardo Redi, et al. | Producer: Alfredo Bini | 35 millimeter, black and white | 88 minutes

A father and son wander through the fields on the outskirts of Rome and encounter a talking raven, who instructs them with his theses on Marxism and religion. But his theories meet with incomprehension. The tale of two Franciscan monks sent forth by St. Francis of Assisi to preach to the "big birds and little birds," or "the hawks and the sparrows," is also lost on the pair. After attending the funeral of Palmiro Togliatti, the respected founder of the Italian Communist Party, the men become hungry and decide to eat the preaching raven, so as not to have to put up with his annoying and apparently useless pearls of wisdom any longer. In a fanciful, funny, and philosophical apology, Pasolini expresses his metaphorical ideas on the crisis of the left and the state of Italian society.

LA TERRA VISTA DALLA LUNA
(THE EARTH SEEN FROM THE MOON),
EPISODE FROM LE STREGHE (THE WITCHES)

Italy 1966 | Screenplay: Pier Paolo Pasolini | Cinematography: Giuseppe Rotunno | Music: Piero Piccioni | Actors: Totò, Ninetto Davoli, Silvana Mangano, Laura Betti, Luigi Leoni, Mario Cipriani | Producer: Dino De Laurentiis | 35 millimeter, Technicolor | 31 minutes

Ciancicato Miao and his son Basciù are mourning the loss of their wife and mother. In their search for a suitable replacement, they happen upon the deaf-mute Assurdina. In order to improve her poor financial situation, Assurdina pretends that she has decided to kill herself due to her impoverishment. While she threatens to hurl herself from the Coliseum walls, father and son collect money for the spectacle from the crowd of curious onlookers. Assurdina slips unexpectedly and plunges to her death, and the money collected must be used to purchase the gravestone. As father and son arrive home, unhappy, Assurdina—miraculously restored to life—comes to meet them and serves them their meal. "Living or dead—it amounts to the same thing," proclaims the closing title of the film, which echoes the comical world of the silent film and elements of folk- and fairytale.

CHE COSA SONO LE NUVOLE?
(WHAT ARE THE CLOUDS?),
EPISODE FROM CAPRICCIO ALL'ITALIANA

Italy 1967 | Screenplay: Pier Paolo Pasolini | Cinematography: Tonino Delli Colli | Music: Song "Così sono le nuvole" by Domenico Modugno and Pier Paolo Pasolini | Actors: Totò, Franco Franchi, Ciccio Ingrassia, Ninetto Davoli, Laura Betti, Adriana Asti, et al. | Producer: Dino De Laurentiis | 35 millimeter, Technicolor | 22 minutes

Once again, Totò and Ninetto, the clowns with no past and no future, are the featured protagonists of a short film, the second part of *Capriccio all'italiana,* whose other segments were directed by Steno, Mauro Bolognini, Pino Zac, and Mario Monicelli. Pasolini took only a week-and-a-half to shoot this film, in which Shakespeare's *Othello* is performed by marionettes. The subproletarian audience interrupts the performance with loud comments and later intervenes physically, killing Iago and Othello. A garbageman collects the puppets' remains and throws them into a heap at the dump. There, for the first time, the astonished puppets glimpse the blue sky with clouds moving through it—the final image of a story of fiction and truth, imprisonment and freedom.

EDIPO RE
(OEDIPUS REX)

Italy 1967 | Screenplay: Pier Paolo Pasolini, adapted from *Oedipus Rex* and *Oedipus at Colonus*, by Sophocles | Cinematography: Giuseppe Ruzzolini | Music: selections from the works of Wolfgang Amadeus Mozart and African, Romanian, Russian, and Japanese folk music | Actors: Franco Citti, Silvana Mangano, Alida Valli, Carmelo Bene, Julian Beck, Pier Paolo Pasolini, Ninetto Davoli, et al. | Producer: Alfredo Bini | 35 millimeter, Technicolor | 104 minutes

According to the Greek tragedy by Sophocles, Oedipus is the son of Laius, the king of Thebes, and his wife Jocasta. When the king receives a prophecy that his son will kill him and then marry his own mother, he has him exposed to the elements and left to die. The child, however, is discovered and grows up far from home. Years later, an oracle presages the terrible events to Oedipus, as well. He leaves Corinth, his home, and makes his way to Thebes. There the prophecy is fulfilled. He kills his father unknowingly and—as a reward for having liberated Thebes from the sphinx—weds the king's widow, his mother. Pasolini's idiosyncratic interpretation of this universal theme has autobiographical features: the prologue takes place in the 1920s, the epilogue in modern Bologna, and the core of the film in ancient Greece.

APPUNTI PER UN FILM SULL'INDIA
(NOTES FOR A FILM ON INDIA)

Italy 1968 | Screenplay: Pier Paolo Pasolini | Cinematography: Federico Zanni, Roberto Nappa, Pier Paolo Pasolini | Producer: Gianni Barcelloni | 35 minutes

In the form of a kind of travel diary, this film depicts the attempt to bring a legend from Indian mythology to the screen. The story deals with a maharaja who sacrifices his body to a tiger cub dying of hunger. Pasolini interviews representative individuals from the country's various social groupings—a maharaja, a chairman of the Communist Party, rich and poor, peasants and workers—about the tale. The film was never made, but precisely the question of impossibility is one of the central themes of this cinematic sketch.

TEOREMA
(THEOREM)

Italy 1968 | Screenplay: Pier Paolo Pasolini, adapted from his novel *Theorem* | Cinematography: Giuseppe Ruzzolini | Music: Wolfgang Amadeus Mozart, Ted Cursen, Ennio Morricone | Actors: Terence Stamp, Silvana Mangano, Massimo Girotti, Anne Wiazemsky, Laura Betti, Andrès José Soublette Cruz, Ninetto Davoli, Susanna Pasolini, et al. | Producer: Franco Rosselini, Manolo Bolognini | 35 millimeter, black-and-white and color (Eastmancolor) | 98 minutes

A stranger who is as handsome as he is mysterious enters the lives of an upper middle-class Milanese industrialist's family. According to Pasolini, the guest "has come to destroy": one by one, he wrenches all the members of the household out of their customary orbits, awakening in each of them energies and emotions whose existence they had never suspected. The spouses, the son, the daughter, and the maid all succumb to his omnipotent sexuality, and the head of the household rejects the construct of an existence based on material prosperity. The visitor's sudden departure leaves behind total confusion and a feeling of emptiness. Pasolini's film examines the influence of the sacred on the everyday life of the bourgeoisie, with truthfulness and lifelong illusions.

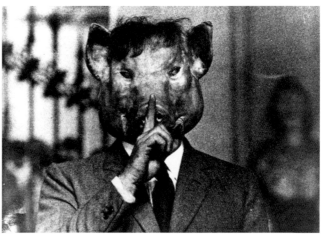

LA SEQUENZA DEL FIORE DI CARTA
(THE PAPER FLOWER SEQUENCE),
EPISODE FROM AMORE E RABBIA (LOVE AND ANGER)

Italy 1968 | Screenplay: Pier Paolo Pasolini, from an idea by Puccio Puci and Piero Badalassi | Cinematography: Giuseppe Ruzzolini | Music: Johann Sebastian Bach, Giovanni Fusco | Actors: Ninetto Davoli, Rochelle Barbieri | Producers: Carlo Lizzani | 35 millimeter, Technicolor | 12 minutes

This film recounts an episode from the Gospel of Matthew, the parable of the innocent fig tree that provokes God's wrath because it does not bear any fruit (Matthew 21:18–19). Holding a big red poppy in his hand, Ninetto Davoli (who seems to be playing himself) ambles lightheartedly along the Via Nazionale in Rome. As he does so, topical and politically explosive images (the Vietnam War, the Cold War) go past like shadows. Completely unaffected by them, Ninetto continues to saunter along, even as the voice of God, "coming from the midst of the traffic," accuses him of ignorance. Finally, his thoughtlessness becomes his undoing, and he must die. As the filmmaker said: "There are moments in history when one cannot be innocent or unaware: not to be aware means to be guilty."

PORCILE
(PIGSTY)

Italy/France 1969 | Screenplay: Pier Paolo Pasolini | Cinematography: Tonino Delli Colli, Armando Nannuzzi, Giuseppe Ruzzolini | Music: Benedetto Ghiglia | Actors: Pierre Clémenti, Jean-Pierre Léaud, Franco Citti, Ninetto Davoli, Alberto Lionello, Anne Wiazemsky, Ugo Tognazzi, Marco Ferreri, Margherita Lozano | Producer: Gian Vittorio Baldi, Gianni Barcelloni | 35 millimeter, color (Eastmancolor), wide-screen | 98 minutes

In two different, parallel strands of the narrative, this film tells the story of two young men who break out of their respective social situations, but ultimately founder and come to macabre ends. One of them lives in an archaic culture, becomes a cannibal, develops a following, and is finally fed to the animals himself as punishment. The other, the son of a German industrialist, pays for his difference when he is devoured by the pigs to which he is drawn by his sodomitic inclinations. In these two enigmatic parables, the film attacks a secularized consumerist society whose power cannot be broken, even by a revolt that violates taboos (cannibalism, sodomy); as Pasolini said of the film: "Society devours its disobedient children."

APPUNTI PER UN'ORESTIADE AFRICANA
(NOTES FOR AN AFRICAN ORESTEIA)

Italy 1969 | Screenplay, Commentary: Pier Paolo Pasolini |
Cinematography: Giorgio Pelloni, Pier Paolo Pasolini | Music:
Gato Barbieri | 16 millimeter, black and white | 63 minutes

As Pasolini and his team search for locations and visual
motifs in Africa, we see take shape before us the attempt
to transfer the *Oresteia* of the Greek tragedian Aeschylus to
the present, in an effort to point out parallels between the
ancient legend and the new political situation in the young
democracies of the "dark continent." Pasolini felt that Africa had arrived at a turning point in its history similar to
that reached by Argos at the time of Orestes. "This could be
Agamemnon," says the commentator about the portrait of a
proud Massai warrior. Footage from Tanzania and Uganda
is combined with texts by Aeschylus and discussions with
students of color at the University of Rome. "My ambition,"
Pasolini declared as early as 1963, "was to invent a new
genre, a film as an ideological and poetic essay."

MEDEA

Italy/France/FRG 1969 | Screenplay: Pier Paolo Pasolini,
adapted from the tragedy by Euripides | Cinematography:
Ennio Guarnieri | Music: Japanese religious music,
Iranian love songs | Musical Direction: Pier Paolo Pasolini,
Che Ringrazia, Elsa Morante | Actors: Maria Callas,
Laurent Terzieff, Massimo Girotti, Giuseppe Gentile,
Margareth Clémenti, Sergio Tramonti, Ninetto Davoli,
Graziella Chiarcossi, et al. | Producer: Franco Rosselini |
35 millimeter, color (Eastmancolor), wide-screen |
110 minutes

This story from the world of ancient legend tells of Medea,
who avenges herself against the unfaithful Jason by killing
his new wife and her own children, fathered by Jason. She
embodies an old, archaic, religious world. Jason, the contemporary hero, by contrast, stands for the new, pragmatic, and
rational one. He has lost the sense of the metaphysical, and
his only concern is success. A love story at bottom, the drama
revolves around the incompatibility of two cultures. "When
I chose this tragedy of barbarity, in which we see a mother
murder her children out of love for a man, what fascinated
me most was the boundless and immoderate quality of her
love," said Pasolini. The film, which is full of sometimes dis-
orienting spatial and temporal leaps, is held together by the
striking and passionate features of Maria Callas, who seems
to be controlling her emotions with visible effort and her last
ounce of strength.

IL DECAMERON
(THE DECAMERON)

Italy/France/FRG 1970 | Screenplay: Pier Paolo Pasolini, after eight novellas from the work of the same name by Giovanni Boccaccio (around 1350) | Cinematography: Tonino Delli Colli | Musical Advisors: Pier Paolo Pasolini, Ennio Morricone | Actors: Franco Citti, Ninetto Davoli, Jovan Jovanovic, Angela Luce, Pier Paolo Pasolini, Giuseppe Zigaina, Silvana Mangano | Producer: Alberto Grimaldi | 35 millimeter, Technicolor | 111 minutes

Taking Boccaccio's collection of novellas as its starting point, the film strings together eight episodes full of opulent sensuality, wit, and slyness, which are loosely connected by a narrative frame. Pasolini remarked: "I was fascinated by the representation of Eros in a human climate which history has hardly ever surpassed, and which is still physically present today (in Naples, in the Middle East)." Out of the jovial temperament and earthy personalities of the amateur actors and the visions of the painter Giotto, played with great power and urgency by Pasolini himself, arises a lively image of the late Middle Ages at the doorstep of the Renaissance—a historical turning point in which Pasolini saw clear parallels with the present. *Il Decameron* constitutes the first part of his *Trilogy of Life.*

I RACCONTI DI CANTERBURY
(CANTERBURY TALES)

Italy 1971 | Screenplay: Pier Paolo Pasolini, from *The Canterbury Tales* by Geoffrey Chaucer (around 1390) | Cinematography: Tonino Delli Colli | Musical Advisors: Pier Paolo Pasolini, Ennio Morricone | Actors: Hugh Griffith, Laura Betti, Ninetto Davoli, Franco Citti, Alan Webb, Josephine Chaplin, Pier Paolo Pasolini, et al. | Producer: Alberto Grimaldi | 35 millimeter, Technicolor | 111 minutes

In the guise of the English poet Geoffrey Chaucer, Pasolini tells stories that the pilgrims of the Middle Ages whispered to one another. They are stories full of miraculous events, graphic eroticism, and comedy, which bring together the lives of the saints, courtly poetry, and bawdy popular tales. Present throughout is a lust for life, but also the thought of death and of the next life. Pasolini said: "When I filmed Canterbury, I was going through an intense crisis. I was very unhappy—I was hardly suited for a trilogy that stood under the sign of merriment, dreams, and humor." As the last bulwark against society's vanishing authenticity, the director saw the natural, "innocent" human body, with its archaic sexuality, its vital force, and its sometimes dark violence.

IL FIORE DELLE MILLE E UNA NOTTE
(ARABIAN NIGHTS)

Italy 1973 | Screenplay: Pier Paolo Pasolini, Dacia Maraini, based on the collection of novellas *Alf Laylah wa-Laylah* | Cinematography: Giuseppe Ruzzolini | Musical Advisor: Ennio Morricone | Actors: Ninetto Davoli, Franco Citti, Franco Merli, Tessa Bouché, Ines Pellegrini, Margareth Clémenti, Abadit Ghidei, et al. | Producer: Alberto Grimaldi | 35 millimeter, Technicolor | 130 minutes (originally 150 minutes, cut by 20 minutes after premiere)

This film is about the pleasure of telling stories. Fifteen episodes from the Eastern fairy tale collection evoke the union of the everyday and the visionary and the boundlessness of dreams. "These stories are connected with the pain I feel at the loss of the past world." They only seem to lack a political dimension: "The world that unfolds there is not the one to which the viewers have been accustomed by consumerist cinema and television. The chief characteristic of these films is that they bring something real to the screen, which the spectator is no longer used to," Pasolini said of the film. During production, Pasolini also made the film *Le mura di Sana'a* (The Walls of Sana'a) about the historical buildings of the capital of Yemen (14 minutes).

SALÒ O LE 120 GIORNATE DI SODOMA
(SALÒ, OR THE 120 DAYS OF SODOM)

Italy/France 1975 | Screenplay: Pier Paolo Pasolini with Sergio Citti, based on the novel *Les cent-vingt journées de Sodome ou l'Ecole du libertinage*, by Donatien-Alphonse-François Marquis de Sade | Cinematography: Tonino Delli Colli | Music: Frédéric Chopin, Carl Orff | Musical Advisor: Ennio Morricone | Actors: Paolo Bonacelli, Aldo Valletti, Umberto Paolo Quintavalle, Giorgio Cataldi, Caterina Boratto, Elsa Di Giorgi, Hélène Surgère, Sonia Saviange, et al. | Producer: Alberto Grimaldi | 35 millimeter, Technicolor | 116 minutes

In his final film, Pasolini evokes a shocking vision of the human obsession with power and barbaric love of destruction in the midst of highly intellectual cultural refinement. The director developed the material from a novel by de Sade and set it in the Republic of Salò, the last refuge of the Italian fascists. A group of sadistic members of the upper middle class stages terrorist rituals of cruelty in a stately villa. Young men and women are humiliated, tortured, and sexually abused. Against the background of a present experienced as hedonistic and corrupted by consumerism, the film presents a period of apocalyptic decline without hope of transformation. The filmmaker remarked after its premiere: "I am a disillusioned man. I was always at odds with society. I fought it, and it persecuted me but also enabled me to achieve a little success. Now I do not love it anymore."

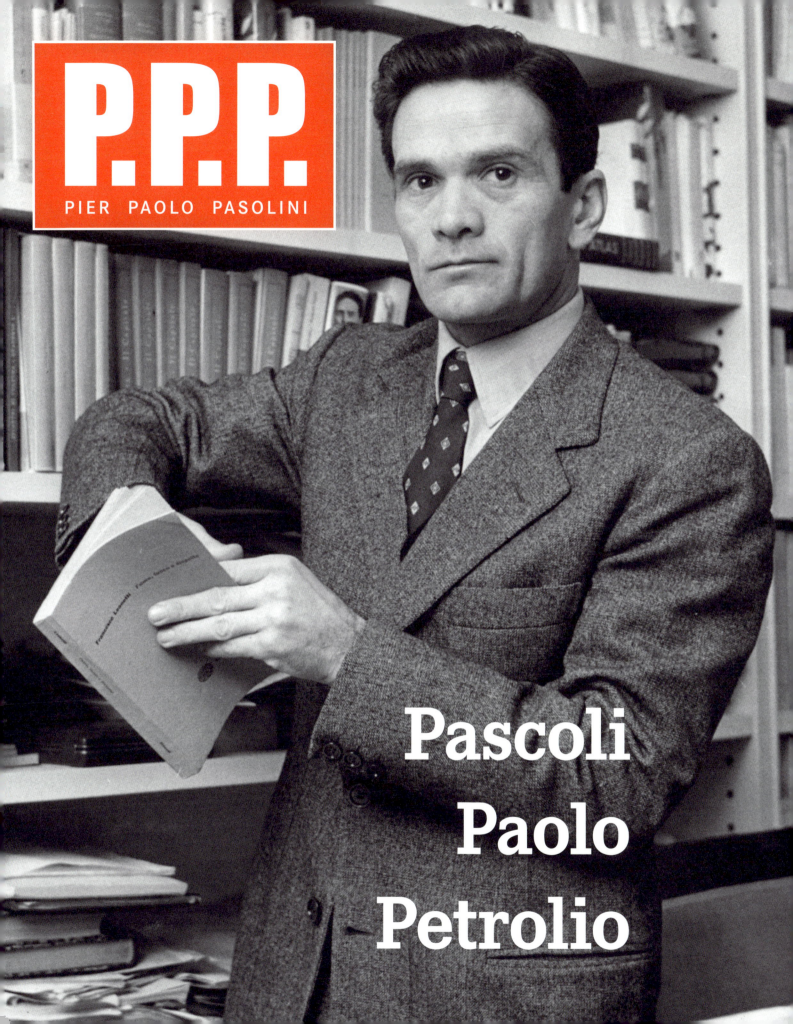

P.P.P.

PIER PAOLO PASOLINI

Pascoli
Paolo
Petrolio

Preceding page
Pasolini in his apartment in the Via Carini, Rome, 1950s

Bibliography

Compiled by Angela Maria Opel

This selected bibliography gives a chronological overview of Pasolini's literary works published in Italian during his lifetime and posthumously, each of which is followed by the English language edition, if available. Secondary literature is organized alphabetically by author and contains international publications. Museum catalogues are listed chronologically by exhibition date.

Works by Pier Paolo Pasolini
Writings 1942–1975

Poesie a Casarsa. Bologna: Libreria Antiquaria Mario Landi, 1942.

Diarii. Casarsa: Pubblicazioni dell'Academiuta, 1945.

I pianti. Casarsa: Pubblicazioni dell'Academiuta, 1946.

Dov'è la mia patria? Casarsa: Pubblicazioni dell'Academiuta, 1946.

Pier Paolo Pasolini and Mario Dell'Arco, eds. *Poesia dialettale del Novecento.* Parma: Guanda, 1952.

Tal cóur di un frut. Nel cuore di un fanciullo. Trecesimo: Edizioni "Friuli," 1953.

Dal diario. Caltanisetta: Sciascia, 1954.

La meglio gioventù. Florence: Sansoni, 1954.

Pier Paolo Pasolini, trans. *Il canto popolare.* Milan: La Meridiana, 1954.

Ragazzi di vita. Milan: Garzanti, 1955.

The Ragazzi. Emile Capouya, trans. Manchester and New York: Carcanet, 1986.

Pier Paolo Pasolini, ed. *Canzoniere italiano: Antologia della poesia popolare.* Parma: Guanda, 1955.

Le ceneri di Gramsci. Milan: Garzanti, 1957.

L'usignolo della Chiesa Cattolica. Milan: Longanesi, 1958.

Una vita violenta. Milan: Garzanti, 1959.
A Violent Life. William Weaver, trans. London: Jonathon Cape, 1968.

Roma 1950: "Diario." Milan: All'insegna del pesce d'oro, 1960.

Donne di Roma. Rome: Il saggiatore, 1960.

Sonetto primaverile. Milan: All'insegna del pesce d'oro, 1960.

Pier Paolo Pasolini, ed. *La poesia popolare italiana.* Milan: Garzanti, 1960.

Pier Paolo Pasolini, trans. Aeschylus, *L'orestiade.* Urbino: Edizioni Urbiante, 1960.

Passione e ideologia: 1948-1958. Milan: Garzanti, 1960.

Accattone. Rome: Edizioni FM, 1961.

La religione del mio tempo. Milan: Garzanti, 1961.

Pier Paolo Pasolini, Bernardo Bertolucci, and Alberto Moravia. *Scrittori della realtà dal VIII al XIX secolo.* Milan: Garzanti, 1961.

Il sogno di una cosa. Milan: Garzanti, 1962.
A Dream of Something. Stuart Hood, trans. London: Quartet, 1988.

Mamma Roma. Milan: Rizzoli, 1962.

L'odore dell'India. Milan: Longanesi, 1962.
The Scent of India. London: Olive Press, 1984.

Pier Paolo Pasolini, trans. Titus Maccius Plautus, *Il vantone. (Miles gloriosus).* Milan: Garzanti, 1963.

Il Vangelo secondo Matteo. Milan: Garzanti, 1964.

Poesia in forma di rosa: 1961-1964. Milan: Garzanti, 1964.

Poesie dimenticate. Udine: Società Filologica Friulana, 1965.

Alì dagli occhi azzurri. Milan: Garzanti, 1965.

Roman Nights and Other Stories. John Shepley, trans. Marlboro, Vt.: Marlboro Press, 1986.

Uccellacci e uccellini. Milan: Garzanti, 1966.

Teorema. Milan: Garzanti, 1968.
Theorem. Stuart Hood, trans. London: Quartet Books, 1992.

Oswald Stack, ed. *Pasolini on Pasolini: Interviews with Oswald Stack.* Bloomington: Indiana University Press, 1969.

Poesie, Milan: Garzanti, 1970.

Pier Paolo Pasolini and Sergio Citti. *Ostia.* Milan: Garzanti, 1970.

Pier Paolo Pasolini, Italo Zannier, Mario De Micheli, and Alfonso Gatto. *Giuseppe Zigaina.* Milan: Bassoli Fotoincisioni, 1970.

Trasumanar e organizzar. Milan: Garzanti, 1971.

Enrico Magrelli, ed. *Con Pier Paolo Pasolini.* Rome: Bulzoni, 1971.

Empirismo eretico. Milan: Garzanti, 1972.
L. K. Barnett, ed. *Heretical Empiricism.* Bloomington: Indiana University Press, 1988.

Calderón. Milan: Garzanti, 1973.

Il padre selvaggio. Turin: Einaudi, 1975.

La nuova gioventù. Turin: Einaudi, 1975.

Le poesie. (anthology including *Le ceneri di Gramsci, La religione del mio tempo, Poesia in forme di rosa, Trasumanar e organizzar*). Milan: Garzanti, 1975.

La Divina Mimesis. Turin: Einaudi, 1975.
Divine Mimesis. Thomas Erling Peterson, trans. Berkeley: Double Dance Press, 1980.

Giorgio Gattei, ed. *Trilogia della vita: Il Decameron; I racconti di Canterbury; Il fiore delle Mille e una notte.* Bologna: Cappeli, 1975.

Scritti corsari. Milan: Garzanti, 1975.

Writings Published after 1975

Nico Naldini, ed. *Lettere, con una cronologia della vita e delle opere.* Turin: Einaudi, 1976.

Lettere luterane. Turin: Einaudi, 1976.
Lutheran Letters. Stuart Hood, trans. Manchester: Carcanet, 1983.

Luciano Serra, ed. *Lettere agli amici (1941–1945): Con un' appendice di scritti giovanili.* Parma: Guanda, 1976.

Luigi Ciceri, ed. *I turcs tal Friúl.* Udine: Rivista Forum Julii, 1976.
Giancarlo Boccotti, trans. *I turchi in Friuli.* Munich and Florence: Istituto Italiano di Cultura, 1980.

Affabulazione - Pilade. Milan: Garzanti, 1977.

Mario Ricci, ed. *Pasolini e "Il setaccio" 1942-1943.* Bologna: Cappeli, 1977.

San Paolo. Turin: Einaudi, 1977.

Gian Carlo Ferretti, ed. *Le belle bandiere: Dialoghi 1960-1965.* Rome: Editori Riuniti, 1977.

—. ed. *Il caos.* Rome: Editori Riuniti, 1979.

Porcile; Orgia; Bestia da stile. Milan: Garzanti, 1979.

Luciano de Giusti, ed. *Il cinema in forma di poesia.* Pordenone: Edizione Cinemazero, 1979.

Graziella Chiarcossi, ed. *Descrizioni di descrizioni.* Turin: Einaudi, 1979.

Nico Naldini and Andrea Zanzotto, eds. *Poesie e pagine ritrovate.* Rome: Lato Side, 1980.

Jean Duflot, ed. *Il sogno del centauro.* Rome: Editori Riuniti, 1983.

Michele Mancini and Giuseppe Perella, eds. *Corpi e luoghi.* Rome: Theorema Edizioni, 1981.

Poems. Norman MacAfee, trans. New York: Vintage, 1982.

Amado mio, preceduto da Atti impuri. Milan: Garzanti, 1982.

Sette poesie e due lettere. Vicenza: La Locusta, 1985.

Cesare Segre, ed. *Il portico della morte.* Rome: Associazione "Fondo Pier Paolo Pasolini," 1988.

Teatro. Milan: Garzanti, 1988.

Petrolio. Turin: Einaudi, 1992.
Petrolio. Ann Goldstein, trans. New York: Pantheon, 1997.

Giovanni Falaschi, ed. *I dialoghi.* Rome: Editori Riuniti, 1992.

Nico Naldini, ed. *Un paese di temporali e di primule.* Parma: Guanda, 1993.

Marco Antonio Bazzocchi, ed.; introduction by Pier Paolo Pasolini. *Antologia della lirica pascoliana.* Turin: Einaudi, 1993.

Graziella Chiarcossi and Walter Siti, eds. *Bestemmia. Tutte le poesie.* Milan: Garzanti, 1993.

Nico Naldini, ed. *Vita attraverso le lettere.* Turin: Einaudi, 1994.

Walter Siti, ed. *Storie della città di Dio. Racconti e cronache romane 1950–1966.* Turin: Einaudi, 1995.
—. ed. *Stories from the City of God: Sketches and Chronicles of Rome 1950–1966.* Marina Harss, trans. New York: Handsel Books, 2003.

Achille Millo, Eugenio Montale, and Pier Paolo Pasolini. *Conversazioni con Montale e Pasolini.* Rome: Poesia 8, 1996.

Roberto Roversi, ed. *Su Pier Paolo Pasolini. Interventi di Alfredo Antonaros* (containing the previously unpublished *La sua gloria).* Bologna: Pendragon, 1996.

Tullio Kezich, ed. *I film degli altri.* Parma: Guanda, 1996.

Walter Siti and Silvia De Laude, eds. *Pasolini – Le opere. Romanzi e racconti,* vol. 1: *1946–1961.* Milan: Mondadori, 1998.

—. eds. *Pasolini – Le opere. Romanzi e racconti,* vol. 2: *1962–1975.* Milan: Mondadori, 1998.

Il padre selvaggio (The Savage Father). Pasquale Verdicchio, trans. Toronto: Guernica, 1999.

Walter Siti and Silvia De Laude, eds. *Pasolini – Le opere. Saggi sulla letteratura e sull'arte.* Milan: Mondadori, 1999.

—. eds. *Pasolini – Le opere. Saggi sulla politica e sulla società,* Milan: Mondadori, 1999.

Walter Siti and Franco Zabagli, eds. *Per il cinema.* Mondadori, 2001.

Walter Siti and Silvia De Laude, eds. *Pasolini – Le opere. Teatro.* Milan: Mondadori, 2001.

Walter Siti, ed. *Tutte le poesie.* Milan: Mondadori, 2003.

Secondary Literature

Kathy Acker. *Mein Leben, mein Tod. Die Geschichte des Pier Paolo Pasolini.* Munich: Heyne, 1987.

Associazione "Fondo Pier Paolo Pasolini," ed. *Pier Paolo Pasolini. Un cinema di poesia.* Rome: Associazione "Fondo Pier Paolo Pasolini," 1988.

—. *Pier Paolo Pasolini: A Future Life.* Rome: Associazione "Fondo Pier Paolo Pasolini," 1989.

Zygmunt Baranski, ed. *Pasolini: Old and New Studies.* Dublin: Four Courts Press, 1999.

Dario Bellezza. *Pasolinis Tod.* Freiburg: Beck und Glückler, 1985.

Antonio Bertini. *Teoria e tecnica del film in Pasolini.* Rome: Bulzoni, 1979.

Laura Betti. *Le regole di un'illusione. I film, il cinema.* Rome: Associazione "Fondo Pier Paolo Pasolini," 1991.

Laura Betti, ed. *Pasolini. Cronaca giudiziaria, persecuzione, morte.* Milan: Garzanti, 1977.

Laura Betti and Sergio Vecchio, eds. *Pier Paolo Pasolini. Une vie futur.* Rome: Fondo Pier Paolo Pasolini, 1987.

Camilla Blechen. "Der Zeichner Pier Paolo Pasolini." *Frankfurter Allgemeine Zeitung,* February 19, 1982.

Detlef Bluemler. "Beharrliches Denken in Bildern. Zeichnungen von Pier Paolo Pasolini im Münchner Kunstverein." *Vorwärts,* July 29, 1982.

Johanna Borek, ed. *Gramsci, Pasolini. Ein imaginärer Dialog.* Vienna: Verlag für Gesellschaftskritik, 1987.

Franco Brevini, ed. *Per conoscere Pasolini.* Milan: Mondadori, 1981.

Giuliano Briganti. *Italian Mannerism.* London: Thames & Hudson, 1962.

Michael Caesar and Peter Hainesworth, eds. *Writers and Society in Contemporary Italy.* New York: St. Martin's Press, 1984.

Italo Calvino. "Les Romans de Pasolini," in Maria Antonietta Macciocchi, ed., *Pasolini: Séminaire dirigé par Maria Antonietta Macciocchi.* Paris: Grasset, 1980.

Giuseppe Conti Calabrese. *Pasolini e il sacro.* Milan: Jaca Book, 1994.

Luciano de Giusti. *Effetto Cinema 6: I film di Pier Paolo Pasolini.* Rome: Gremese Editore, 1983.

Gualtiero de Santi. Maria Lenti, and Roberto Rossini, eds. *Perché Pasolini.* Florence: Guaraldi, 1978.

Franca Faldini and Goffredo Fofi, eds. *L'avventurosa storia del cinema italiano.* Milan: Feltrinelli, 1981.

—. *Pier Paolo Pasolini. Lichter der Vorstädte. Die abenteuerliche Geschichte seiner Filme.* Karl Baumgartner and Ingrid Mylo, trans. Hofheim: Wolke, 1986.

Adelio Ferrero. *Il cinema di Pier Paolo Pasolini.* Venice: Marsilio, 1977.

Gian Carlo Ferretti. *Pasolini. L'universo orrendo.* Rome: Editori Riuniti, 1976.

Hal Foster, ed. *The Anti-Aesthetic. Essays on Postmodern Culture.* Port Townsend, WA: Bay Press, 1983.

Peter H. Göpfert. "Das Grün der Traubenkerne für Medea. Pier Paolo Pasolini Zeichnungen in Hannover." *Die Welt,* June 15, 1982.

Robert S. C. Gordon. *Pasolini. Forms of Subjectivity.* Oxford: Clarendon Press, 1996.

Naomi Greene. *Pier Paolo Pasolini. Cinema as Heresy.* Princeton: Princeton University Press, 1990.

Armin Halstenberg. "Remythologisierung von Bildern," in Hans Günther Pflaum, ed., *Jahrbuch Film 1982/1983.* Munich: Hanser, 1982.

Raimund Hoghe. "Kontaktversuche," *Die Zeit,* February 12, 1982.

Peter W. Jansen and Wolfram Schütte (eds.). *Reihe Film, vol. 12: Pier Paolo Pasolini.* Munich and Vienna: Hanser, 1977.

Christoph Klimke, ed. *Kraft der Vergangenheit. Zu Motiven der Filme von Pier Paolo Pasolini.* Frankfurt am Main: S. Fischer, 1988.

—. *Der Sünder. Fragen an Pier Paolo Pasolini.* Berlin: Vis a Vis, 1985.

Friedrich Kröhnke. *Gennariello könnte ein Mädchen sein. Essays über Pasolini.* Frankfurt am Main: Materialis Verlag, 1983.

Wolfgang Längsfeld. "In privater Offenheit." *Süddeutsche Zeitung,* July 23, 1982.

Ben Lawton. "The Storytellers' Art," in Andrew S. Horton and Joan Magretta, eds., *Modern European Filmmakers and the Art of Adaptation.* New York: Ungar, 1981.

Jutta Lindner. *Pasolini als Dramatiker.* Frankfurt am Main: Lang, 1981.

Millicent Marcus. *Italian Film in the Light of Neorealism.* Princeton: Princeton University Press, 1986.

Dacia Maraini, Alberto Moravia, Ettore Scola, and Enzo Siciliano. "Pier Paolo Pasolini: Témoignages." *Cahiers du Cinéma,* nos. 268/269, July/August 1976.

Lino Micchiè. *Il cinema italiano degli anni sessanta.* Venice: Marsilio, 1975.

Alberto Moravia. "L'ideologia di Pasolini," in Pier Paolo Pasolini, *Raggazzi di vita.* Milan: Garzanti, 1976.

—. "Il dovere di morire," in Laura Betti, ed., *Pasolini. Cronaca giudiziaria, persecuzione, morte.* Milan: Garzanti, 1977.

Nico Naldini. *In den Feldern Friauls. Die Jugend Pasolinis.* Stuttgart: ComMedia und Art Verlag, 1987.

—. *Pasolini. Una vita.* Turin: Einaudi, 1986.
—. Maja Pflug, trans. *Pier Paolo Pasolini. Eine Biographie.* Berlin: Wagenbach, 1991.

Achille Bonito Oliva and Giuseppe Zigaina. *Disegni e pitture di Pier Paolo Pasolini.* Basel: Balance Rief S. A., 1984.

Maurizio Ponzi. *Pier Paolo Pasolini – Rainer Werner Fassbinder.* Hamburg: Europäische Verlagsanstalt, 1996.

Johannes Reiter and Giuseppe Zigaina, eds. *Pier Paolo Pasolini. Zeichnungen und Gemälde.* Basel: Balance Rief SA, 1982.

Sam Rohdie. *The Passion of Pier Paolo Pasolini.* Bloomington: Indiana University Press, 1995.

Patrick A. Rumble and Bart Testa, eds. *Pier Paolo Pasolini: Contemporary Perspectives.* Toronto: University of Toronto Press, 1994.

Patrick A. Rumble. *Allegories of Contamination: Pier Paolo Pasolini's Trilogy of Life.* Toronto: University of Toronto Press, 1995.

Barth David Schwartz. *Pasolini: Requiem.* New York: Pantheon Books, 1992.

Otto Schweitzer. *Pasolini.* Reinbek/Hamburg Rowohlt, 1986.

Mona Sehrawy. "The Suffering Text: *Poesie a Casarsa* and the Agony of Writing." *The Italianist,* no. 5, 1985.

Klaus Semsch. *Literatur und Ideologie Marxistisches Weltbild und dichterische Kreativität im lyrischen Werk Pier Paolo Pasolinis.* Essen: Verlag Die Blaue Eule, 1989.

Enzo Siciliano. *La vita di Pasolini.* Milan: Rizzoli, 1978.

—. *Pasolini. Leben und Werk,* Christel Galliani, trans. Weinheim: Beltz und Gelberg, 1980.

—. *Pasolini. A Biography.* New York: Random House, 1982.

Kristian Sotriffer. "Mit dem Saft der Mohnblume." *Presse,* December 6, 1982.

Piero Spila. *Pier Paolo Pasolini.* Rome: Gremese Editore, 1999.

—. *Pier Paolo Pasolini.* Martina Mitsch, trans. Rome: Gremese Editore, 2002.

V. L. "Selbstporträt im Fieberzustand. Pier Paolo Pasolini im Kunstmuseum Basel." *Neue Zürcher Zeitung,* September 15, 1982.

Maurizio Viano. A Certain Realism: Making Use of Pasolini's Film Theory and Practice. Berkeley: University of California Press, 1993.

Karin von Hofer. *Funktionen des Dialekts in der italienischen Gegenwartsliteratur. Pier Paolo Pasolini.* Munich: Fink, 1971.

Konstantin Wecker. "Elegie für Pasolini." Hans Stempel and Martin Ripkens, eds., *Das Kino im Kopf.* Zurich: Arche, 1984.

Hermann H.Wetzel, ed. *Pier Paolo Pasolini.* Mannheim: MANA, 1984.

Hans Peter Wilberg. *Das Evangelium nach Matthäus. Mit Aufnahmen aus dem gleichnamigen Film von Pier Paolo Pasolini.* Gütersloh: Gütersloher Verlagshaus Gerd Mohn, 1965.

Paul Willemen, ed. *Pier Paolo Pasolini.* London: The British Institute, 1977.

Karsten Witte. "Pasolini. Der Traum von einer bösen Sache." *Pier Paolo Pasolini. Wiederkehr eines Mythos?* Frankfurt am Main: Theater am Turm, 1983.

Giuseppe Zigaina, ed. *Pier Paolo Pasolini. I disegni 1941–1975.* Milan: Edizioni di Vanni Scheiwiller, 1978.

—. *Pasolini e la morte.* Venice: Marsilio, 1987.

—. *Pasolini und der Tod. Mythos, Alchemie und Semantik des glänzenden Nichts. Eine Studie.* Munich: Piper, 1989.

—. *Hostia.* Venice: Marsilio, 1995.

—. *Pasolini e il suo teatro: "Senza anteprime né prime né repliche."* Venice: Marsilio, 2003.

Exhibition Catalogues

Pier Paolo Pasolini. Zeichnungen und Gemälde. Johannes Reiter, ed. Freunde der Deutschen Kinemathek Berlin. Basel: Balance Rief SA, 1982.

L'univers esthètique de Pasolini. Chapelle de la Sorbonne, Paris: Persona, 1984.

Pier Paolo Pasolini. "… mit den Waffen der Poesie …." Akademie der Künste. Berlin, 1994.

Pier Paolo Pasolini oder Die Grenzüberschreitung / Organizzar il trasumanar. Giuseppe Zigaina and Christa Steinle, eds. Neue Galerie am Landesmuseum Joanneum. Venice: Marsilio, 1995.

Pier Paolo Pasolini. Un poeta d'opposizione. Laura Senserini, ed. Teatro di Roma. Milan: Skira, 1995.

Pier Paolo Pasolini: Palabra de corsario. Círculo de Bellas Artes. Madrid, 2005

P. P. P. – Pier Paolo Pasolini and Death. Bernhart Schwenk and Michael Semff, ed. Pinakothek der Moderne. Ostfildern-Ruit: Hatje Cantz Verlag, 2005.

This catalogue is published in conjunction
with the exhibition
P. P. P.–Pier Paolo Pasolini and Death
November 17, 2005–February 5, 2006
Pinakothek der Moderne, Munich

Catalogue

Edited by
Bernhart Schwenk and Michael Semff

Copyediting
Eugenia Bell

Editorial coordination
Tas Skorupa

Translations
Paul Aston, Matthew Gaskins, Jim Gussen,
Ben Letzler, Laura Schleussner

Graphic design, production, and typesetting
rose apple · design, Berlin/Rose Apple, Yvonne Krug
chezweitz, Berlin/Detlef Josef Weitz,
Benjamin Meyer-Krahmer

Typeface
Minion, Corporate, Bodoni

Reproductions
Pallino cross media GmbH, Ostfildern-Ruit

Paper
Design offset, 120g/m², 1.25 volume

Binding
Buchbinderei Thomas Müntzer, Bad Langensalza

Printed by
Dr. Cantz'sche Druckerei, Ostfildern-Ruit

Published by
Hatje Cantz Verlag
Senefelderstrasse 12
73760 Ostfildern-Ruit
Germany
Tel. +49 711 4405-0
Fax +49 711 4405-220
www.hatjecantz.com

Hatje Cantz books are available internationally
at selected bookstores and from the following distribution
partners:

USA/North America - D.A.P., Distributed Art Publishers,
New York, www.artbook.com

UK - Art Books International, London,
sales@art-bks.com

Australia - Tower Books, Frenchs Forest (Sydney),
towerbks@zipworld.com.au

France - Interart, Paris, commercial@interart.fr

Belgium - Exhibitions International, Leuven,
www.exhibitionsinternational.be

Switzerland - Scheidegger, Affoltern am Albis,
scheidegger@ava.ch

For Asia, Japan, South America, and Africa, as well as
for general questions, please contact Hatje Cantz directly
at sales@hatjecantz.de, or visit our homepage **www.
hatjecantz.com** for further information.

ISBN 3-7757-1633-5 (English edition)
ISBN 3-7757-1632-7 (German edition)

Printed in Germany

Cover illustration
Pasolini on the set of
Il fiore delle mille e una notte, 1973

Pages 14–15
Pier Paolo Pasolini's funeral, 1975

Exhibition

Curators
Bernhart Schwenk, Michael Semff
in collaboration with Giuseppe Zigaina

Curatorial assistant
Angela Maria Opel

Research assistant
Carolin Angerbauer

Exhibition design
chezweitz, Berlin/Detlef Josef Weitz,
Benjamin Meyer-Krahmer, Rose Apple
mit Birgit Noij, Dominic Müller, Michael Kunter

Exhibition installation
Dietmar Stegemann

Media
Lars Raffelt

Conservator
Katrin Schroeter

Exhibition office
Birgit Keller, Gertraud Stark

Registrars
Simone Kober, Gertraud Stark

Public relations
Gina Becker, Tine Nehler
with Bianca Henze, Angela Seemüller

Events
Andrea Pophanken, Barbara Siebert

Information office
Susanne Kudorfer
with Anja Zechel

The exhibition was made possible by a substantial grant
from Gruppo Euromobil per la Cultura and Antonio,
Fiorenzo, Gaspare, and Giancarlo Lucchetta. Gruppo
Euromobil has been sponsoring international art exhibitions
for many years, and most importantly provided support
for Giuseppe Zigaina's Pasolini research.

Photo Credits

ANSA: pp. 10, 33
Deborah Beer: pp. 69, 104, 185, 199
Divo Cavicchioli: pp. 9, 69, 193
Elio Ciol: p. 77
L'Espresso: p. 107
Federico Garolla: p. 6 (1st from right); p. 7 (1st and 2nd
from left, 5th and 6th from left); p. 68
Michael Kunter: endpapers
Angelo Novi: p. 9 (1st and 2nd from left); pp. 33, 45,
46, 51, 55, 66 (ills. 2, 3, 4); 67, 68, 70 (ills. 1 and 2);
pp. 72, 76, 78, 95, 111, 191, 192, 195
Marilù Parolini: p. 196
Dino Pedriali: p. 117
Angelo Pennoni: jacket and cover image, pp. 66, 71,
73, 74, 75, 96, 145
Christoph Petras: cover using a photograph
by Angelo Pennoni
Paul Ronald: pp. 47, 76
Mario Tursi: p. 10 (1st from left), pp. 36, 39, 49, 60,
65, 71, 72, 73, 77, 78, 86, 101, 162, 198